Vol. XV No. 1

Adult Bible Class
Large-Print Edition

WINTER QUARTER December 2023, January, February 2024

Editorial 2

Living in Christ

UNIT I: New Life in Christ

Dec. 3—To Live Is Christ—Phil. 1:12-26 4
Dec. 10—Counting All Things Loss—Phil. 3:7-21 9
Dec. 17—Learning Contentment—Phil. 4:4-18 14
Dec. 24—The Light of Christmas (Christmas)—John 1:1-5; Eph. 5:1-2, 6-14 19

UNIT II: Transformed Lives in Christ

Dec. 31—Chosen in Christ—Eph. 1:3-14 24
Jan. 7—God's Workmanship—Eph. 2:1-10 29
Jan. 14—The Household of God—Eph. 2:11-22 34
Jan. 21—A High Calling—Eph. 4:1-16 39
Jan. 28—God-Honoring Families—Eph. 5:21—6:4 43

UNIT III: Lives Worthy of Christ

Feb. 4—Spiritual Armor—Eph. 6:10-24 47
Feb. 11—The Supremacy of Christ—Col. 1:15-28 51
Feb. 18—Complete in Christ—Col. 2:6-19 55
Feb. 25—A Plea for Christlike Forgiveness—Phm. 1:4-21 59
                Paragraphs on Places and People 63
                Daily Bible Readings 64

Editor in Chief: Kenneth Sponsler

Union
Gospel
Press

Edited and published quarterly by
THE INCORPORATED TRUSTEES OF THE
GOSPEL WORKER SOCIETY
UNION GOSPEL PRESS DIVISION
Rev. W. B. Musselman, Founder
Price: $6.09 per quarter*
*shipping and handling extra

ISBN 978-1-64495-408-9

This material is part of the "Christian Life Series," copyright © 2023 by Union Gospel Press. All rights reserved. No portion of this publication may be reproduced in any form or by any means without written permission from Union Gospel Press, except as permitted by United States copyright law. Edited and published quarterly by The Incorporated Trustees of the Gospel Worker Society, Union Gospel Press Division. Mailing address: P.O. Box 301055, Cleveland, Ohio 44130-0915. Phone: 216-749-2100. www.uniongospelpress.com

EDITORIAL

We Are Alive!

BY MATTHEW ROBINSON

Scripture has a strong word for the state of humanity apart from Christ: *dead*. Not merely sick. Not merely misguided or in need of correction. Dead.

Praise God that Scripture has an even stronger word for the state of those who are in Christ: *alive*! This eternal life that God has breathed into dead sinners encompasses not only our future life in heaven but also our life here and now.

This quarter we will seek to understand the nature of that new life in Christ. We will explore biblical principles for living it out as well as practical ways we can apply those principles today.

Unit I focuses on the nature of our new life in Christ, showing the stark contrast between our old life and our new life. Before, we were dead in our sins and unable to please God in anything we did (Eph. 2:1-3). Now, we can please Him in both life and death (lesson 1). We are able to rejoice even in our greatest trials, because Christ's glory has become our greatest goal (Phil. 1:12-26).

Everything that we considered "gain" in the past is now "loss" when compared with knowing Christ and His power in our lives (Phil. 3:7-21; lesson 2). The sinful passions we once held in the highest esteem, we now understand are doomed for destruction. What we once considered "glory," we now recognize as "shame" (vs. 19).

Before, we were governed by fear; now, we are governed by peace (Phil. 4:4-18; lesson 3). God has given us free access to His throne of grace that we might cultivate that peace with Him through prayer (vss. 6-7). Even in our trials we can pray "with thanksgiving"; as we depend on the Lord, He will strengthen us for every circumstance (vs. 13). Because "to live is Christ" (1:21), we can be content in Him. A believer in the worst of circumstances is infinitely better off than an unbeliever in the best of circumstances (cf. Ps. 37:16; 73:1-18).

How is all this possible for human hearts that were formerly imprisoned in darkness? The answer is in the Christmas message (lesson 4): In the incarnate Son, the light came down from heaven and scattered the darkness (John 1:1-5). For all who do not receive Him, exposure to the light leads to judgment. But for all who do receive Him, the light of Christ's holiness will purify our hearts. As we expose our lives to that light, the darkness that remains in us will have nowhere to hide. It must flee from the righteous Judge (Eph. 5:1-2, 6-14).

We might recap unit I this way: our life in Christ has been given to us as a free gift, and God promises to finish the work He has begun in us (Phil. 1:6). But that does not mean we can just sit on the sidelines and watch. In fact, Paul instructs us to "work out [our] salvation with fear and trembling," even as God Himself is the one working in us (2:12-13).

Unit II focuses on several key principles we need to keep in mind as we seek to live transformed lives in Christ. The first principle we need to understand is *why* God has chosen to give us new life in Christ (lesson 5). Ephesians

1:3-14 tells us the reason: that we might be "to the praise of his glory" (vs. 12; cf. vss. 6, 14). Glorifying God involves becoming "holy and without blame before him" (vs. 4), that is, being transformed into the image of Christ (Rom. 8:29).

Lesson 6 (Eph. 2:1-10) shows us our responsibility as children of God to respond to His grace. Our transfer from death to life had nothing to do with any works that we did (vs. 9), but as living children of God we are to walk in obedience to our Father by doing the good works that He Himself has lovingly prepared for us to do (vs. 10).

Our growth in holy living does not happen in isolation. It happens within the church (lesson 7). God has broken down every excuse for hostility between Christians by basing His salvation of each one of us on the blood of Christ, not on our own merit. Therefore, we are called to be transformed into the image of Christ not only as individuals, but also as a unified body of believers (Eph. 2:11-22).

Christ gives the church spiritual leaders to aid in this process of growth (Eph. 4:1-16; lesson 8). Ultimately, the role of these leaders is not to take all the work of ministry onto themselves, but rather to *equip* all the saints for that ministry (vs. 12). He has uniquely gifted each Christian so that we will build one another up in love.

Within this broader church context, Paul singles out the family unit as one of the most important contexts for spiritual growth (lesson 9). For those of us with families, mutual self-sacrifice in marriage and patient instruction of children are two primary means of growth in Christ (Eph. 5:21—6:4).

Finally, in unit III, keeping those guiding principles in mind, we turn to some practical instruction for living our new life in Christ.

Lesson 10 (Eph. 6:10-24) reminds us that living for Christ is not only a path to walk; it is a battle to fight. This battle

is a spiritual one—not against people but against demonic powers and sin (vss. 10-12). That means our armor needs to be spiritual. Paul tells us what armor we need in verses 13-20.

Even as we put on those pieces of spiritual armor, let's not forget the goal of the armor: keeping us focused on the hope of the gospel (Col. 1:15-28; lesson 11) and rooted in Christ (2:6-19; lesson 12).

Finally, one of the primary ways we imitate Christ is by forgiving one another (Phm. 1:4-21; lesson 13). When Paul asks Philemon to forgive his runaway slave by receiving him back as a brother, he expects that Philemon will do even more than he asks (vs. 21). When we truly understand how much God has forgiven us, we will gladly forgive one another as well (cf. Matt. 18:21-35).

LESSON 1   DECEMBER 3, 2023

SCRIPTURE LESSON TEXT

PHIL. 1:12 But I would ye should understand, brethren, that the things *which happened* unto me have fallen out rather unto the furtherance of the gospel;

13 So that my bonds in Christ are manifest in all the palace, and in all other *places;*

14 And many of the brethren in the Lord, waxing confident by my bonds, are much more bold to speak the word without fear.

15 Some indeed preach Christ even of envy and strife; and some also of good will:

16 The one preach Christ of contention, not sincerely, supposing to add affliction to my bonds:

17 But the other of love, knowing that I am set for the defence of the gospel.

18 What then? notwithstanding, every way, whether in pretence, or in truth, Christ is preached; and I therein do rejoice, yea, and will rejoice.

19 For I know that this shall turn to my salvation through your prayer, and the supply of the Spirit of Jesus Christ,

20 According to my earnest expectation and *my* hope, that in nothing I shall be ashamed, but *that* with all boldness, as always, *so* now also Christ shall be magnified in my body, whether *it be* by life, or by death.

21 For to me to live *is* Christ, and to die *is* gain.

22 But if I live in the flesh, this *is* the fruit of my labour: yet what I shall choose I wot not.

23 For I am in a strait betwixt two, having a desire to depart, and to be with Christ; which is far better:

24 Nevertheless to abide in the flesh *is* more needful for you.

25 And having this confidence, I know that I shall abide and continue with you all for your furtherance and joy of faith;

26 That your rejoicing may be more abundant in Jesus Christ for me by my coming to you again.

NOTES

To Live Is Christ

Lesson Text: Philippians 1:12-26

Related Scriptures: Acts 28:11-16, 30-31; I Corinthians 3:5-9;
II Corinthians 5:1-9; II Timothy 4:6-8

TIME: A.D. 60-61   PLACE: from Rome

GOLDEN TEXT—"In nothing I shall be ashamed, but that with all boldness, as always, so now also Christ shall be magnified in my body, whether it be by life, or by death" (Philippians 1:20).

Lesson Exposition

PUTTING CHRIST'S CAUSE BEFORE COMFORT—Phil. 1:12-14

New ministry for Paul (Phil. 1:12-13). As Paul wrote to the Philippian church, he desired to motivate them to faithful Christian living and service. He pointed to the example of his own life. It is easy for Christians to get discouraged when life gets difficult. Paul knew all about those kinds of pressures and temptations.

As Paul was visiting Jerusalem, he was arrested and imprisoned. Even though the Roman authorities acknowledged that he was innocent, they did not release the apostle. Eventually Paul appealed his case to Caesar, the Roman emperor. After a long voyage to Rome, during which he nearly lost his life, Paul arrived at the capital. There he was placed under house arrest (Acts 21—28).

In looking back on the whole unjust, humiliating ordeal, Paul could easily have become disillusioned and bitter. Instead, he looked past his personal pain to the progress that the gospel had made through his suffering. Instead of using his own comfort as the standard for evaluating his situation, Paul measured his experiences in terms of how they furthered the cause of Christ.

As Paul examined the circumstances of his confinement, he realized that the Lord had opened up for him an exciting and strategic new ministry that he never could have anticipated. The soldiers who guarded Paul were members of the elite Praetorian Guard, who were assigned to the imperial palace. Paul thus had a mission field in his own house, a captive audience of strategically positioned men who took turns monitoring the apostle.

Paul used the opportunity to tell the soldiers about Christ, thus reaching an audience that the Christian congregations most likely would never have encountered.

New motivation for the brethren (Phil. 1:14). No doubt the first reaction of other Christians to the news of Paul's imprisonment was discouragement. If this leader of the church, the indomitable pioneer missionary, was no longer able to lead, what future did the church have?

As word of Paul's impact on Rome began to circulate, discouragement gave way to renewed courage. Other

Christians, seeing that Paul did not shrink back in the face of hostility, became more bold in their witness.

PUTTING CHRIST'S PURPOSE BEFORE PRIDE—Phil. 1:15-18

A mixed reaction (Phil. 1:15-16). As Paul considered the numerous Christians who had been motivated through his example to increase their ministry efforts, he was aware that they were divided into two distinct groups. On the one hand, some of those who were boldly preaching about Christ did so for the wrong reasons. They were opposed to Paul, possibly because of his emphasis on God's grace rather than the law.

In addition to this possible theological motivation, these preachers were motivated by selfishness. They were envious of Paul, so they used the occasion to promote themselves.

Paul concluded that these men were not preaching Christ sincerely, with pure motives, but from a contentious spirit. Their envy of Paul prompted them to try to kick him when he was down. They assumed that Paul would feel pained when he heard of people shifting their loyalty from him to them. In thinking this, they were supposing that Paul functioned by the same selfish motivations that drove them.

On the other hand, some believers rose to the challenge of Paul's imprisonment by lovingly filling the gap that the apostle left. They ministered out of goodwill.

A modest response (Phil. 1:17-18). Paul refused to fight fire with fire. He knew well that his opponents were trying to add pain to his imprisonment. He nevertheless chose to focus on the positive aspects of the situation.

For one thing, those who supported Paul were demonstrating their love for both him and Christ.

As Paul saw other believers choosing to stand as he did for the gospel, he rejoiced in what God had done through his example.

Paul also focused on what even poor intentions could accomplish for the cause of Christ. His opponents may have intended to hurt him by their hypocritical preaching, but they still managed to get the word out about Christ. Although Paul was undoubtedly wounded by their antagonism, he refused to let his feelings become his primary concern. Instead, he rejoiced in the fact that Christ was being preached by others, that the gospel was being heard by the unsaved, and that God's cause was advancing.

PUTTING CHRIST'S DUTY BEFORE DESIRE—Phil. 1:19-26

Confidence in Christ (Phil. 1:19-20). The reason Paul could swallow his own pride and rejoice even when his opponents preached Christ out of impure motives was that he placed his confidence in Christ.

By quoting the words of Job 13:16, in which Job anticipated his eventual deliverance by God, Paul demonstrated that he was placing his situation into God's hands.

Despite the painful circumstances and the threatening prospects that Paul faced, his major focus was not on getting out of the difficulty. Instead, Paul earnestly wanted to respond to the challenge in such a way that he would not bring shame to the cause of Christ. It would be tempting to back away from his commitment to Christ in order to avoid condemnation by Caesar. That, however, would be to deny the Lord out of timidity and fear. Paul determined rather to stand boldly and speak for Christ.

Paul was keenly conscious that his appearance before the imperial court was giving him a larger platform for proclaiming Christ. Whether he was released or executed, the message of Christ would become more widely known than ever before.

Commitment to Christ (Phil. 1:21-22). Paul summarized the driving force in his life in a memorable affirmation: "For to me to live is Christ, and to die is gain." Paul was so consumed by his commitment to Christ that for him, living meant Christ.

At the same time, physical death for Paul was nothing short of gain. If he died because of his commitment to Christ, he would be giving his life for the One who had already given His own life for sinners. In addition, to be absent from the physical body would mean that Paul would be present with his Lord (II Cor. 5:8). To die, therefore, would be gain.

As Paul looked at it, both life and death had advantages. On the one hand, continued life provided additional opportunities to serve the Lord he loved. On the other hand, physical death would usher him into a deeper fellowship in the presence of the Lord.

Considerations for Paul (Phil. 1:23-24). Paul admitted to the Philippians that he had a hard time deciding which of the alternatives he preferred. He candidly said that his personal desire would be to depart this life and to be with Christ. Death, as Paul saw it, was like breaking up a campsite and leaving for home. To leave this earth and come into the presence of Christ would be better by far for Paul personally.

As attractive as that prospect was, Paul also desired the other alternative. His love for other Christians, specifically the Philippians, was so deep that he felt constrained to focus on their need.

Paul sensed that the believers needed his ministry to establish and sustain them in their Christian lives. If he had only his own welfare to consider, to die would be his desire, but in light of the needs of other Christians, Paul felt that he had to live and serve as long as possible.

Continuance of ministry (Phil. 1:25-26). Paul became convinced that God's purpose for him was to continue ministering to the believers. He had a renewed vision of the calling that God had for him—to continue to labor to bring the Philippians to spiritual maturity.

Instead of complaining about the long and painful process that he had endured, Paul contemplated the benefit his continued ministry would bring the Philippians. He anticipated that it would produce great rejoicing among those who loved him and had prayed for him. His imprisonment had prompted the believers to intensify their prayers, and answered prayer builds stronger confidence in God.

—*Daniel J. Estes.*

QUESTIONS

1. Why did Paul view his imprisonment in a positive way?
2. How did Paul's imprisonment open strategic new doors for the ministry of the gospel?
3. Why did some of the Christians become more bold in their witness?
4. How did Paul's opponents try to attack him?
5. Why did Paul refuse to take offense at those who tried to hurt him?
6. What did Paul focus on instead of his painful circumstances?
7. What was Paul's motto, which summarized the key focus of his life?
8. If Paul had considered only his personal benefit, what would he have preferred to do?
9. Why was Paul convinced that he would continue to live?
10. How would Paul's release benefit the Philippians?

—*Daniel J. Estes.*

PRACTICAL POINTS

1. If we are God's children, we can be sure that our trials will bring glory to Him (Phil. 1:12).
2. Our boldness in witnessing will encourage others to proclaim the gospel (vss. 13-14).
3. We should rejoice whenever Christ is proclaimed and people respond, even if we suspect that the preaching is not from pure motives (vss. 15-18).
4. The goal of our prayers for our brethren should always be that Christ will be magnified (vss. 19-20).
5. Our lives should be so Christ-centered that even the possibility of imminent death does not overwhelm us as long as His will is done (vss. 21-24).
6. We will have joy in ministering to others if our desire is to see them progress in the faith and experience the blessings of knowing and serving Christ (vss. 25-26).

—Jarl K. Waggoner.

RESEARCH AND DISCUSSION

1. How would you describe Paul's attitude toward suffering (cf. II Cor. 4:15-18)?
2. Does rejoicing that Christ is proclaimed mean that we should support or encourage all who are proclaiming Him (Phil. 1:15-18)? Explain.
3. We may not know precisely how to pray for someone in a given situation, but what are some things we can always pray for people (vss. 19-20)?

—Jarl K. Waggoner.

Golden Text Illuminated

"In nothing I shall be ashamed, but that with all boldness, as always, so now also Christ shall be magnified in my body, whether it be by life, or by death" (Philippians 1:20).

How do you live to please Christ? What is involved in such an approach to life? Our text supplies us with two answers to these questions.

The first answer is a negative one. It is found in these words: "In nothing I shall be ashamed." In other words, living to please Christ means you will not do anything that would cause you to be ashamed in His presence.

Do you desire to have confidence before God? Do you want to live to please Christ? Do not do anything that would cause you to shrink back from His presence.

The second answer to how to please Christ is given in a positive manner. It is found in these words: "Christ shall be magnified in my body." Instead of doing things that will embarrass you in the presence of God, you must wholeheartedly do those things that will exalt Christ. When that is the aim of your life, you will be living to please Christ.

Notice that Paul said that Christ should be exalted with boldness. You should not be timid when it comes to honoring Christ. Glorify Him boldly and confidently.

"By life, or by death" is Paul's way of saying that this was his aim, no matter what the cost. Christ should be exalted in our lives at all costs. Only after your life shows such commitment can you say you are living to please Him.

Living for Christ will cost you something, that is sure. But the reward is great.

—James R. Gordon.

LESSON 2   DECEMBER 10, 2023

Scripture Lesson Text

PHIL. 3:7 But what things were gain to me, those I counted loss for Christ.

8 Yea doubtless, and I count all things *but* **loss for the excellency of the knowledge of Christ Jesus my Lord: for whom I have suffered the loss of all things, and do count them** *but* **dung, that I may win Christ.**

9 And be found in him, not having mine own righteousness, which is of the law, but that which is through the faith of Christ, the righteousness which is of God by faith:

10 That I may know him, and the power of his resurrection, and the fellowship of his sufferings, being made conformable unto his death;

11 If by any means I might attain unto the resurrection of the dead.

12 Not as though I had already attained, either were already perfect: but I follow after, if that I may apprehend that for which also I am apprehended of Christ Jesus.

13 Brethren, I count not myself to have apprehended: but *this* one thing *I do,* forgetting those things which are behind, and reaching forth unto those things which are before,

14 I press toward the mark for the prize of the high calling of God in Christ Jesus.

15 Let us therefore, as many as be perfect, be thus minded: and if in any thing ye be otherwise minded, God shall reveal even this unto you.

16 Nevertheless, whereto we have already attained, let us walk by the same rule, let us mind the same thing.

17 Brethren, be followers together of me, and mark them which walk so as ye have us for an ensample.

18 (For many walk, of whom I have told you often, and now tell you even weeping, *that they are* **the enemies of the cross of Christ:**

19 Whose end *is* destruction, whose God *is their* belly, and *whose* glory *is* in their shame, who mind earthly things.)

20 For our conversation is in heaven; from whence also we look for the Saviour, the Lord Jesus Christ:

21 Who shall change our vile body, that it may be fashioned like unto his glorious body, according to the working whereby he is able even to subdue all things unto himself.

NOTES

Counting All Things Loss

Lesson Text: Philippians 3:7-21

Related Scriptures: Matthew 16:24-28; Romans 9:30—10:4;
I Thessalonians 1:2-10; Hebrews 12:1-2; I Peter 1:3-9

TIME: A.D. 60-61   PLACE: from Rome

GOLDEN TEXT—"But what things were gain to me, those I counted loss for Christ" (Philippians 3:7).

Lesson Exposition

STRIVING FOR EXCELLENCE—Phil. 3:7-11

Finding true gain (Phil. 3:7-8). Before Paul was saved, his life was marked by credentials of many kinds. Paul spoke of some of these in verses 4 through 6. To the people in his society, Paul had achieved at the highest level in every significant category of life.

In human terms, Paul had ample reason to be proud of his pedigree and performance. Nevertheless, as he looked at all those things he could claim, he realized that in God's kingdom they were worth nothing. In fact, they were less than nothing; they were loss, for they had stood in the way of Paul's surrender to Christ.

When Paul trusted Christ as his Saviour, he made a dramatic, life-altering calculation. He compared all that he had achieved by his own efforts with what Christ could accomplish in and through him. As Paul viewed his life from the perspective of God's values, he decided to give up all those things for which he had lived. He gave them up as loss so that he could gain Christ.

As Paul came to realize, personal assets can easily become spiritual liabilities if they blind us to the ultimate value of knowing Christ. Instead of living for his own pride or for the applause of others, Paul chose to focus his life on the truly excellent goal of the knowledge of Christ Jesus, his Lord.

When he was converted, Paul began a personal relationship with Christ, but he aspired to know Christ intimately. He was saved in a moment, but it would take a lifetime to get to know Christ well. Knowing Christ made every other goal look like garbage.

Finding true righteousness (Phil. 3:9). Before Paul was saved, he had been a strict adherent of the Old Testament Law of Moses. In fact, he had prided himself on the fact that he was blameless with respect to the righteousness that is in the law (vs. 6). As a Christian, however, Paul learned that his own righteousness acquired through keeping the law is not true righteousness at all.

In Christ, Paul possessed true righteousness, the righteousness that comes from God through faith in Christ.

This genuine righteousness is a gift of God. When a person receives Christ as his Saviour, God also gives him the righteousness of Christ. Believers' sins were in fact debited to Christ's account at the Cross. But just as vital is the truth that Christ's righteousness has also been placed in the account of believers.

Finding true intimacy (Phil. 3:10-11). In verse 10 Paul returned to the ultimate goal of his life—to truly know Christ intimately. Intimacy does not come cheap in human relationships, and the same is true in getting to know Christ well. Deep intimacy comes from sharing the full range of life's pleasures and pains.

Paul recognized that intimacy is built on identification. On the one hand, knowing Christ meant coming to experience the power of Christ's resurrection, which enables the believer to live a new life of victory over sin (Rom. 6:4-11). On the other hand, knowing Christ involves pain. We know Him better when we suffer righteously as He did.

STRIVING WITH EXERTION—
Phil. 3:12-16

Reaching forward (Phil. 3:12-13). The road to spiritual excellence requires exertion. As Paul spoke of his own path to greater knowledge of God, he described it as an active pursuit of godliness. To come to know God intimately, Paul had to reach toward that goal. That meant that he had to keep moving forward spiritually.

Paul's lofty goal did not blind him to his own spiritual condition. The closer he drew to God, the more he realized his own sinfulness. Paul was painfully aware that he was imperfect, a sinner saved only by God's grace. He did not challenge the Philippians from an attitude of superiority or perfection; rather, he admitted frankly that he had not yet attained the goal of intimate knowledge of God. He was certain that he was saved, but he knew that he had far to go before he would reach his potential for Christ.

To move forward, Paul had to keep focusing on the future. He refused to look back in the rearview mirror of life to all his supposed credentials before he was saved, nor did he let guilt and regrets for past actions shackle him and impede his spiritual progress.

Pressing upward (Phil. 3:14). Paul continued his athletic picture in verse 14. Like a runner, Paul pressed toward, or pursued, the mark—knowing Christ and being like Him. He was not distracted by the crowd, and he did not compare himself to the other contestants in the race. All his attention was riveted on reaching the finish line.

As Paul looked ahead to the prize, he anticipated an honor that far surpassed what any human official could give. God Himself was the race official, and He would call Paul before Him to give him the prize. The commendation "Well done, good and faithful servant" (Matt. 25:23) was worth all the effort that Paul put into pursuing the knowledge of God.

Walking onward (Phil. 3:15-16). After referring to himself individually in verses 7 through 14, Paul included the Philippians in verses 15 and 16. He wanted them to join him in his single-minded pursuit of God. Intimate knowledge of God should mark every Christian life, not just the lives of a pious elite.

Paul admitted in verse 12 that he himself was not yet perfect, but apparently some of the Philippians were not so modest. With gentle irony Paul urged them to have the same mind as he did. Instead of priding themselves on how far they had come already, they needed to keep focused on the final goal of truly knowing God.

At the same time, Paul encouraged the believers to keep up the good qualities that were present in their lives. The Christian life is won in the routine of faithful obedience to God. Steady progress over time is the key to eventual victory.

STRIVING IN EXPECTATION—Phil. 3:17-21

Following a good pattern (Phil. 3:17). We often hear people say, "Do as I say, not as I do." Those words are used to excuse actions that do not live up to the person's instruction to others. As Paul challenged the Philippians to press on for Christ, he practiced what he preached. Without being egotistical, Paul urged them to follow his example. Because Paul himself was following Christ, those who followed his good pattern would be led into true godliness.

Forsaking a bad pattern (Phil. 3:18-19). The Philippians, like Christians today, had to choose what pattern to follow. On the one hand, they could follow the example of Paul, Timothy, and Epaphroditus as they lived out genuine Christianity. On the other hand, there were also people who were enemies of the cross of Christ. Paul had warned the Philippians previously about following bad examples (vs. 2). As Paul wrote, he wept at the thought of the peril that Christ's enemies posed for the Philippians.

The good news of the gospel is that we are saved by grace, not by keeping the law. Those who insisted that the law was still binding upon Christians were resisting what Christ accomplished on the cross.

Instead of glorying in what Christ did, they continued to focus on the law. They prided themselves on keeping the dietary regulations, the rite of circumcision, and all the rest of the ordinances of the law. In doing this, they were placing their minds on earthly things rather than on heavenly things. They were spiritual underachievers and were bad examples for Christians to follow.

Focusing on the best pattern (Phil. 3:20-21). Paul concluded his challenge to the Philippians by centering their attention on Christ. Although they were living on earth, they needed to remember that their first loyalty was to their Lord.

Christians on earth have a dual citizenship. In Christ they have become citizens of heaven. They look to heaven for the return of Christ to earth. When He comes, He will change mortal, physical bodies into immortal, spiritual bodies like His own. Christians, therefore, must live on the basis of their identity in Christ, not simply as humans residing on earth.

—*Daniel J. Estes.*

QUESTIONS

1. What did Paul consider loss for the sake of Christ?
2. What goal did Paul choose to make the ultimate focus of his life?
3. How did Paul, as a Christian, define true righteousness?
4. What potentially surprising thing did Paul include as part of truly knowing Christ?
5. How did Paul reach forward rather than look back?
6. What prize was Paul seeking in his Christian life?
7. What is the key to achieving victory in the Christian life?
8. Why did Paul tell the Philippians to follow him?
9. In what ways were the enemies of Christ resisting what He had accomplished on the cross?
10. How are Christians citizens of two worlds?

—*Daniel J. Estes.*

PRACTICAL POINTS

1. One who truly knows Christ as Saviour and Lord cannot cherish the world's values (Phil. 3:7-8).
2. Righteousness is not the result of fleshly effort but of faith (vs. 9).
3. The Christian life is not a life of ease but a guarantee of suffering (Phil. 3:10-11; cf. II Tim. 3:12).
4. We must never become complacent in our spiritual walk (Phil. 3:12-14).
5. We should seek out examples of godly living who will provide us with encouragement to live up to Christ's calling (vss. 15-17).
6. A godless lifestyle proves that a person is an enemy of Christ, regardless of what he might say (vss. 18-19).
7. As citizens of heaven, Christians should never become too much at home in this world but rather should long for Christ's return (vss. 20-21).

—Jarl K. Waggoner.

RESEARCH AND DISCUSSION

1. How has your perspective on life changed since you became a Christian? What things do you now count "loss for Christ" (Phil. 3:7)?
2. Did Paul teach that a Christian can reach a state of sinless perfection (vss. 12, 15)? Explain.
3. What marks someone as a worthy example to follow (vs. 17)? What characterizes those who are "enemies of the cross of Christ" (vs. 18)?
4. In what sense are Christians citizens of both heaven and earth (vs. 20)? What responsibilities accompany this dual citizenship?

—Jarl K. Waggoner.

Golden Text Illuminated

"But what things were gain to me, those I counted loss for Christ" (Philippians 3:7).

In today's golden text, Paul emphasizes the change of direction his life had taken. He does this by saying that he was not just neutral about his past, but rather that he considered all the religious qualifications he had just listed (vss. 4-6) to be "loss."

A familiar and true maxim is that the only way to emerge out of a bad lifestyle is to replace it with a better passion or ideal. And this is certainly what happened with Paul. His past looked to him like "dung" (vs. 8) when compared to the riches of God's grace he had found in Christ. Of course, he recognized that it was not his wisdom or willpower that had brought about this change. It was all due to God's saving power (cf. Eph. 2:1-9).

In the context of Philippians 3, what are the things Paul has most in mind when he speaks of gain turning to loss? First, he was considering what it takes to be declared righteous in God's sight. Paul warned of the danger posed by the Judaizers, who would require circumcision in order to be saved. If anyone had cause to boast about their legalistic qualifications, it was Paul (vss. 1-4). But he realized that the only righteousness that could save him was Christ's righteousness through faith in His saving work (vs. 9).

Second, Paul was thinking about what it was that truly empowered righteous living. And the clear answer is that true godliness comes through the resurrection power that raised Christ from the dead (vs. 10). To be a follower of Christ by God's power until we see Him face to face is the way of everlasting gain.

—Stephen H. Barnhart.

LESSON 3   DECEMBER 17, 2023

Scripture Lesson Text

PHIL. 4:4 Rejoice in the Lord alway: *and* again I say, Rejoice.

5 Let your moderation be known unto all men. The Lord *is* at hand.

6 Be careful for nothing; but in every thing by prayer and supplication with thanksgiving let your requests be made known unto God.

7 And the peace of God, which passeth all understanding, shall keep your hearts and minds through Christ Jesus.

8 Finally, brethren, whatsoever things are true, whatsoever things are honest, whatsoever things *are* just, whatsoever things *are* pure, whatsoever things *are* lovely, whatsoever things *are* of good report; if *there be* any virtue, and if *there be* any praise, think on these things.

9 Those things, which ye have both learned, and received, and heard, and seen in me, do: and the God of peace shall be with you.

10 But I rejoiced in the Lord greatly, that now at the last your care of me hath flourished again; wherein ye were also careful, but ye lacked opportunity.

11 Not that I speak in respect of want: for I have learned, in whatsoever state I am, *therewith* to be content.

12 I know both how to be abased, and I know how to abound: every where and in all things I am instructed both to be full and to be hungry, both to abound and to suffer need.

13 I can do all things through Christ which strengtheneth me.

14 Notwithstanding ye have well done, that ye did communicate with my affliction.

15 Now ye Philippians know also, that in the beginning of the gospel, when I departed from Macedonia, no church communicated with me as concerning giving and receiving, but ye only.

16 For even in Thessalonica ye sent once and again unto my necessity.

17 Not because I desire a gift: but I desire fruit that may abound to your account.

18 But I have all, and abound: I am full, having received of Epaphroditus the things *which were sent* from you, an odour of a sweet smell, a sacrifice acceptable, wellpleasing to God.

NOTES

Learning Contentment

Lesson Text: Philippians 4:4-18

Related Scriptures: II Corinthians 9:1-15; 12:7-10

TIME: A.D. 60-61   PLACE: from Rome

GOLDEN TEXT—"Rejoice in the Lord alway: and again I say, Rejoice" (Philippians 4:4).

Lesson Exposition

REJOICING IN CHRIST'S PRESENCE—Phil. 4:4-5

In his challenge in Philippians 4:4, Paul made it crystal clear how he wanted the Philippians to respond. By repeating the word "rejoice" twice and by placing it as the first word and the last word of the exhortation, Paul made emphatic his call to joy. He wanted to be sure that his message of rejoicing would not be overlooked or misunderstood.

Many times people derive their joy from pleasant circumstances. When life seems to be going well, they are happy, but when the situation becomes difficult, their joy evaporates. The joy that Paul urged, however, was not conditioned by circumstances; rather, he exhorted his readers to rejoice in the Lord *always*. Their joy was to be found not in what they could achieve by their efforts or in what life presented to them but in Christ's constant commitment to them. Circumstances may be very painful and disappointing, but Christ will always be there for His people with love, help, and faithful support. As the Philippians faced hard times, they could find joy in the Lord.

Just as pressure can dampen joy, so it can produce friction among people. Paul therefore went on to exhort the Philippians to manifest "moderation," or gentleness, to others (vs. 5). Just as they were to rejoice in the Lord at all times, so they were to be gentle to all people. Once again, this response runs counter to human nature.

REJOICING IN CHRIST'S PEACE—Phil. 4:6-9

Being guarded by the peace of God (Phil. 4:6-7). Difficult times not only tend to rob us of joy; they can also remove our peace. Before we know it, we can become consumed with worry and anxiety. Because of this, Paul instructed the Philippians in how they could win against worry.

Speaking negatively, Paul commanded, "Be careful for nothing" (vs. 6). He was not urging a careless lack of concern or a passive lack of action. Instead, he was counseling them not to be consumed by a concern that was beyond their control. By assuming responsibility for factors that were not rightfully theirs, they would only be afflicted by false guilt, which creates unnecessary anxiety.

Paul followed this with a positive command. He told the Philippians to pray about everything. This command was very specific. Paul defined *when* they should pray—in everything (every circumstance). He taught them *how* to pray—with thanksgiving. And he instructed them *what* to do—let their requests be made known to God.

God's peace surpasses all human understanding. Anxious thoughts can cloud our thinking so that we see no way out of our problems. God's peace, however, is more than enough for any situation in life. No worry can withstand the power of God's peace.

God's peace also provides security, guarding our hearts, the seat of desires, and our minds, or thoughts. This security comes through Christ Jesus. The key to victory over worry is facing life's pains in the light of God's provision. Recognizing God's power liberates from fear. Understanding God's purpose delivers from despair. Appreciating God's wisdom releases from doubt. God's strong, sensitive care is the root of peace, which defeats worry in our lives.

Glorifying the God of peace (Phil. 4:8-9). After Paul defined how Christians can experience God's peace, he discussed how they can keep rejoicing in peace. The key to continuing peace is in the mind. Paul therefore taught the Philippians how to maintain a mind that pleases God.

First, he challenged them to examine their minds. Specifically, Paul wanted the Philippians to evaluate the content of their thoughts. In order to experience God's continuing joy, they needed to set their minds on those things that God values. God wants His people to think about things that are true, honest, just, pure, lovely, and of good report. These are the kinds of things that should occupy the minds of Christians.

Second, Paul exhorted the Philippians to elevate their minds. In our world, people often applaud actions and attitudes that are superficial, impure, and ungodly. Christians need to set their sights higher. They should focus their attention on what God regards as virtuous and praiseworthy. Christians should not settle for the mediocre thinking that characterizes popular culture; rather, they should let excellence mark all their actions, their values, and their thinking.

Third, Paul urged the Philippians to exercise their minds (vs. 9). In the Bible, thinking and doing are always linked together. Changed thinking should always result in a transformed life.

REJOICING IN CHRIST'S PROVISION—Phil. 4:10-18

Contribution by the Philippians (Phil. 4:10). Paul ended his letter to the Philippians on a warm, personal note. After teaching them to rejoice in Christ's presence and peace, Paul related how he himself was rejoicing in Christ's provision.

Paul had no doubt about the love of the Philippians for him. Nevertheless, the arrival of their gift was like the bursting of spring flowers into bloom. It was a fresh, tangible expression of their love and concern for the apostle. This outpouring of love caused Paul to rejoice in the Lord greatly.

Contentment in every condition (Phil. 4:11-12). As Paul thanked the Philippians for their gift, he was careful to reassure them of his contentment. He did not want them to think that his thanks was an indirect request for more.

Paul makes clear in verse 12 that he knew what it was like to abound and to enjoy a full life. Through his life experiences, however, he had come to learn the full range of financial states. In addition to knowing how to abound, he also knew how to be abased. He had endured times of hunger and need, as well as times of plenty. Through these various situations, Paul had learned to be content in whatever state God placed him.

The Stoic philosophy in Paul's day defined contentment as self-discipline that enabled a person to rise above life's circumstances. The Stoic attitude of self-sufficiency led to pride. For Christians, contentment comes from joyful dependence upon God, regardless of the circumstances. By drawing upon God's sufficient resources, Christians can have peace even during the most challenging times of life.

Confidence in Christ's strength (Phil. 4:13). Because Paul had learned to be content everywhere and in all things, he could say confidently, "I can do all things through Christ which strengtheneth me." Whether his future meant prosperity or poverty, pain or gain, Paul knew that he could find his strength in God's inexhaustible power. He was not facing the challenge alone, but with God. He did not depend on his personal resources or even on other Christians, such as the Philippians, but on the Lord. The Lord would enable Paul to face the uncertain future with confidence and contentment.

Commendation to the Philippians (Phil. 4:14-16). Paul felt somewhat awkward about accepting the Philippians' gift. He certainly had a legitimate need that they had met. At the same time, his confidence was in the Lord, not in them. In maintaining his dependence on the Lord, however, Paul did not want to sound ungrateful for what the Philippians had done for him.

Consequently, Paul complimented the Philippians on their good gift to him (vs. 14). He was afflicted with a genuine need, and they had answered with genuine help. God had provided His resources through the responsive hands of the Philippians. They were channels of God's blessings and provision for Paul.

The gift Paul had received was really only the most recent in a long list of generous acts by the Philippian church. Right from the beginning of the congregation, they had given Paul financial assistance so that he could take the gospel to the people of Thessalonica.

Consequence of giving (Phil. 4:17-18). Once again, Paul assured the Philippians that what he really wanted for them was spiritual fruit. Using the language of banking, Paul stated his desire that their financial investment in his ministry might yield a high return of rewards and blessings for them.

Paul himself had received the gift they had sent by Epaphroditus. This ample gift supplied Paul's need abundantly. Moreover, their gift was an acceptable and pleasing sacrifice to God. By giving to God's servant, Paul, they were really giving to the Lord Himself.

—*Daniel J. Estes.*

QUESTIONS

1. How did Paul emphasize his challenge to rejoice?
2. What attitude were the Philippians to maintain toward other people?
3. How did Paul teach the Philippians to win against worry in their lives?
4. How does God protect His people from anxiety?
5. What kinds of thoughts should dominate a Christian's mind?
6. How had the Philippians demonstrated their love and concern for Paul?
7. How did Paul explain the Christian concept of contentment?
8. Why was Paul able to be confident in the face of earthly challenges?
9. Why were the Philippians especially worthy of gratitude for their financial support?
10. How did Paul describe the Philippians' gift?

—*Daniel J. Estes.*

PRACTICAL POINTS

1. If we know the Lord as our Saviour, we always have reason to rejoice (Phil. 4:4).
2. The promise of the Lord's return should motivate us to live exemplary lives before the world (Phil. 4:5; cf. I John 3:2-3).
3. Humble, heartfelt prayer is the cure for worry (Phil. 4:6-7).
4. If we focus our thoughts on things that are virtuous, the actions that follow are much more likely to be in accord with God's will (vss. 8-9).
5. The key to contentment in any circumstance is knowing that God is in complete control of our lives (Phil. 4:10-13; cf. II Cor. 12:7-10).
6. Those who give to supply the needs of others bring God's blessing upon themselves as well as upon the recipients (Phil. 4:14-18).

—Jarl K. Waggoner.

RESEARCH AND DISCUSSION

1. In practical terms, what does it mean to "rejoice in the Lord alway" (Phil. 4:4)? How is this possible?
2. Why do we sometimes worry? Is worry a sin? Explain.
3. How can we ensure that we think about good, praiseworthy things (vs. 8)? What steps can we take?
4. Why is Paul's contentment such a powerful example for us (4:11-12; cf. 1:12-14)?
5. What are some of the reasons we become discontented?
6. Is Paul's statement in 4:13 an open-ended promise with no limits? Explain.

—Jarl K. Waggoner.

Golden Text Illuminated

"Rejoice in the Lord alway: and again I say, Rejoice" (Philippians 4:4).

The verse before us calls us to focus on the Lord instead of our circumstances. What a challenge! It is natural for us to look at our surroundings and then react. Often this happens without our even thinking about it.

Peter's actions illustrate the point of our text. Jesus came to the disciples by walking on water (Matt. 14:25). He helped calm the disciples' fears first by identifying Himself (vss. 26-27). We then read this remarkable account: "Peter answered him and said, Lord, if it be thou, bid me come unto thee on the water. And he said, Come. And . . . Peter . . . walked on the water, to go to Jesus. But when he saw the wind boisterous, he was afraid; and beginning to sink, he cried, saying, Lord, save me" (vss. 28-30). Jesus rescued him and then rebuked him for his lack of faith (vs. 31).

Do not overlook Peter's remarkable act here: he actually walked on water! He did so as long as he was trusting in the Lord. When he took his eyes off Jesus, he started to sink.

Has the presence of Jesus made a difference in your life? Is your focus on yourself and your unpleasant circumstances, or is it on Christ?

Can you say with Paul, "Nay, in all these things we are more than conquerors through him that loved us" (Rom. 8:37)? Are you convinced that nothing "shall be able to separate us from the love of God, which is in Christ Jesus our Lord" (vs. 39)? Without such conviction, the storms of life will overwhelm you. Fix your eyes on Jesus today.

—James R. Gordon.

LESSON 4   12/26/23   DECEMBER 24, 2023

Scripture Lesson Text

JOHN 1:1 In the beginning was the Word, and the Word was with God, and the Word was God.

2 The same was in the beginning with God.

3 All things were made by him; and without him was not any thing made that was made.

4 In him was life; and the life was the light of men.

5 And the light shineth in darkness; and the darkness comprehended it not.

EPH. 5:1 Be ye therefore followers of God, as dear children;

2 And walk in love, as Christ also hath loved us, and hath given himself for us an offering and a sacrifice to God for a sweetsmelling savour.

6 Let no man deceive you with vain words: for because of these things cometh the wrath of God upon the children of disobedience.

7 Be not ye therefore partakers with them.

8 For ye were sometimes darkness, but now *are ye* light in the Lord: walk as children of light:

9 (For the fruit of the Spirit *is* in all goodness and righteousness and truth;)

10 Proving what is acceptable unto the Lord.

11 And have no fellowship with the unfruitful works of darkness, but rather reprove *them.*

12 For it is a shame even to speak of those things which are done of them in secret.

13 But all things that are reproved are made manifest by the light: for whatsoever doth make manifest is light.

14 Wherefore he saith, Awake thou that sleepest, and arise from the dead, and Christ shall give thee light.

NOTES

Adult Bible Class   19

The Light of Christmas

(Christmas)

Lesson Text: John 1:1-5; Ephesians 5:1-2, 6-14

Related Scriptures: I John 1:1-7; John 13:34-35; Colossians 3:12-17

TIMES: eternity past; A.D. 60   PLACES: heaven; from Rome

GOLDEN TEXT—"The Word was made flesh, and dwelt among us, (and we beheld his glory, the glory as of the only begotten of the Father,) full of grace and truth" (John 1:14).

Lesson Exposition

THE CREATOR—John 1:1-5

Jesus' preexistence (John 1:1-2). The Christmas story does not begin at Bethlehem. With the words "In the beginning," John purposely pointed his readers back to Creation in order to make his point: Jesus was already in existence at the time of the Creation.

Calling Jesus the "Word" is significant and unique in the Gospels. It stresses the value of Christmas. John used it to present Jesus as the divine Son of God. He knew it would be meaningful for both his Jewish and his Gentile readers.

Jews would associate the term with its Greek Old Testament usage. In that version of the Old Testament, the Greek term indicated God's Word and its source—the divine intellect.

The Gentiles associated *logos,* the Greek term for "Word" used in John 1:1, with the ultimate rationale behind the universe. To them this word spoke of beginnings, so they too would understand that John was connecting Jesus with the One who started time. John then emphasized the plurality of God by describing Jesus' presence *with* God at the beginning (vs. 2).

Jesus' preincarnate work (John 1:3-5). We think of God the Father as the Creator of the universe—and He is—but these verses also show the role of His Son (cf. Col. 1:15-16). Jesus' birth was the Creator inserting Himself into the world He created. Hebrews begins: "God, who at sundry times and in divers manners spake in time past unto the fathers by the prophets, hath in these last days spoken unto us by his Son, whom he hath appointed heir of all things, by whom also he made the worlds" (1:1-2).

Life also came from Jesus. It is not said to have been created, because it already existed in the Godhead at the time of Creation. The important truth here is probably centered in the provision of eternal life, but the phrase is not limited to that. Jesus is the source of all forms of life, including eternal life.

Not only do we have life through Jesus Christ, but we also have light along with it. In this context, light refers to spiritual understanding and moral insight. These qualities enable people to know God and grasp the revelation He presents about Himself in His Word. And yet, light is again practically synonymous with life itself (John 1:4; 8:12).

Those who reject the light of Jesus have neither spiritual understanding nor eternal life (cf. Rom. 1:21; Eph. 4:18).

THE CHALLENGE—Eph. 5:1-2, 6-7

Imitators of God (Eph. 5:1-2). God's Son coming to earth has great implications for us: He showed us what God is like. The Greek word for "followers" means *imitators*. We have often observed how little children imitate their parents, and in just the same way we are supposed to imitate our Heavenly Father. The verb "be" at the beginning of the command is a present-tense verb in the original language, here signifying continuous action. Our imitation is to be daily and lifelong.

As imitators of God, we are to walk in love. In the New Testament, "walking" is a reference to how we live. Our lives are to be characterized by love. That is the kind of love Jesus showed in His death on the cross. Jesus' love is a self-sacrificing love. He gave Himself for us. In other words, no one took His life from Him; He willingly gave it for our benefit.

Paul said Jesus' offering of Himself was a fragrant scent to God. When Israel offered their sacrifices, the smoke ascended upward, as if going into the presence of God and causing Him to be pleased with the aroma.

"Love" in verse 2 translates *agape*—a love that is unconditional and steadfast, not shallow and temporary. We must have unwavering, wholehearted love toward others, just as Christ exercises a deep and faithful love toward us. And His love is like His Father's, which made Christmas possible: He loved the world so much that He sent His Son to be born of Mary (John 3:16).

Sons of disobedience (Eph. 5:6-7). Paul warned believers not to be deceived by vain, empty, worthless words. When he said, "Because of these things cometh the wrath of God upon the children of disobedience," he may have been referring back to verse 5, where several things are mentioned as being part of the lifestyle of those who do not know God. Those who were practicing these corrupt behaviors are defined as "children of disobedience." Paul also may have had in mind what he mentioned in 4:14, where he referred to false doctrine meant to deceive.

Both these matters bring God's wrath. They originate in those who dishonor Christ, those whom Paul said believers should have nothing to do with. Unbelievers, along with their evil actions, are objects of God's wrath.

THE CHANGE—Eph. 5:8-14

Walking as children of light (Eph. 5:8-10). This is the second of three "walk" commands. Verse 2 says to walk in love, and verse 15 to walk cautiously in true wisdom. The birth of Christ signaled the start of God's concentrated attack on the kingdom of darkness. The Light of Christmas can never be extinguished. In fact, because of the Child of Light born in the stable, there now are multitudes of "children of light" (vs. 8). As they walk in the light, the denizens of darkness are invariably defeated. Paul wrote to the Thessalonian believers, "Ye are all the children of light, and the children of the day: we are not of the night, nor of darkness" (I Thess. 5:5). The startling fact is that we did not just *walk* in darkness as unbelievers; we *were* darkness!

People are not basically good, as some would have us believe. Those who are ignorant of God's Word are identified with the evil of this world and thus are the embodiment of darkness. All that changes, however, when that natural darkness is dispelled by the light of the truth as found in the gospel of Christ.

Exposing the works of darkness (Eph. 5:11-12). Paul gave a dual command in verse 11—one negative and one positive. First, we should not have fellowship with the unfruitful works of darkness. That reflects back to the thought of not being partners with those who live in darkness. We are to avoid walking in the ways of darkness because we are now children of light. The idea of having fellowship is very similar to the idea of being partners.

To be unfruitful is to be barren, yielding no profit or reward. Sinful living bears nothing profitable or worthwhile. It does not benefit the person who indulges in it. It is pleasant for a season, but it yields only death.

The second command is to reprove those unfruitful works of darkness. It is not enough just to abstain from sin; we are also to expose it for what it really is.

"Just as the light shines into darkness and exposes what is hidden, so the light of Christ, through a believer, should shine into the darkness of sin and expose it for what it is. God needs people who will take an active and vocal stand against sin and permissiveness in all its forms (see Leviticus 19:17). Christians must lovingly speak out for what is true and right" (Osborne, ed., *Life Application Bible Commentary: Ephesians,* Tyndale).

Manifesting by means of light (Eph. 5:13-14). It is impossible to ignore the darkness that surrounds us daily, but we must not participate in it. During the Christmas season, unbelievers often seem more receptive to the light of the gospel. We should use the extraordinary opportunities at Christmastime to introduce people to the Christ whom the holiday celebrates.

Since we are to walk as children of light, it is the light within us that will expose the darkness around us. To manifest something means to render it apparent, that is, to make it clearly seen and understood. We do not have to participate in activities of darkness in order to expose them. All we need to do is consistently live as those who know and understand God's standards and expectations. That means there will be many times when certain things are taking place and we must take a stand and not be part of them.

The poetic quote Paul included in Ephesians 5:14 probably came from a hymn, based on statements found in Isaiah 26:19, 51:17, 52:1, and 60:1. It seems to express the truth that when sin has been exposed and a person becomes a believer, he awakens from his spiritual darkness, arises from his spiritual death, and is given the light of the truth that comes from Jesus Christ.

This Christmas, may we walk in the light and bring Christ's light of salvation to the lost.

—Keith E. Eggert.

QUESTIONS

1. Why did John begin his Gospel with the same words that begin the book of Genesis?
2. Why would both Jews and Gentiles understand that John was connecting Jesus with God the Father?
3. What things does light symbolize in John 1?
4. What does it mean to be followers of the Father?
5. What kind of walk are we to have that imitates that of Jesus?
6. What is said to bring God's wrath on the sons of disobedience?
7. What happens when we walk as "children of light" (Eph. 5:8)?
8. What are the two parts of Paul's dual command about darkness?
9. What does it mean that darkness is unfruitful?
10. What is the ultimate effect of our light shining in the world?

—Keith E. Eggert.

PRACTICAL POINTS

1. Christ reflects the brightness of God's love and exposes the darkness of sin (John 1:1-5).
2. We should be motivated to love others because Christ did the same for us (Eph. 5:1-2).
3. Imitating someone who does not follow God may wrongly influence others (vss. 6-7).
4. Our lives should reflect and illustrate Christ's character, not our own (vss. 8-10).
5. Following Christ reveals the total futility of living any other way (vs. 11).
6. The light of God's Word reveals how we should live for Him (vss. 12-14).

—Anne Adams.

RESEARCH AND DISCUSSION

1. What does it mean to have the light of Christ? Does this mean you know more about God than others? Explain.
2. What does it mean to "walk in love" (Eph. 5:2)? What prevents you from walking as you would like to? What is the most pressing issue you deal with, and how can you best handle it?
3. Does living for Christ upset those who do not do so? Why? How can someone serve God without alienating others? Is that possible to do?
4. Do you know people who openly boast that they follow Christ more closely than others do? How should you respond? Is it your job to correct them?

—Anne Adams.

Golden Text Illuminated

"The Word was made flesh, and dwelt among us, (and we beheld his glory, the glory as of the only begotten of the Father,) full of grace and truth" (John 1:14).

The Christmas holiday celebrates the coming of God to earth. This was Jesus, the Word of God (Rev. 19:13), who was born in the town of Bethlehem. The Word was and is God.

God's Word was not just written words; when Mary gave birth, the Word became flesh—alive in human form! Jesus, the Living Word, dwelled among sinful humans, and they "beheld his glory."

The glory that was evident at the giving of the law was extraordinary, but the glory of Jesus and His grace is far greater (II Cor. 3:7-11)! His glory was incomparable because it was "the glory as of the only begotten of the Father."

The term "grace" refers generally to the many miracles and tender care Jesus showed during His time of ministry on earth. He was not sparing with His acts of mercy; rather He was *full* of grace. So many people received His help that great crowds followed Him (Mark 1:45; 3:20; 4:1; 6:31).

The grace of Jesus that is emphasized also provides an intriguing doctrinal contrast. The Mosaic Law could only condemn (Rom. 7:10-11), but Jesus provides grace that results in eternal life for repentant sinners.

Besides being gracious, Jesus was full of truth. What He said could be trusted.

The Living Word, our Saviour, became flesh at Christmas so that mankind could have hope. Let us rejoice in the wonder of the incarnation!

—Todd Williams.

LESSON 5   DECEMBER 31, 2023

Scripture Lesson Text

EPH. 1:3 Blessed *be* the God and Father of our Lord Jesus Christ, who hath blessed us with all spiritual blessings in heavenly *places* in Christ:

4 According as he hath chosen us in him before the foundation of the world, that we should be holy and without blame before him in love:

5 Having predestinated us unto the adoption of children by Jesus Christ to himself, according to the good pleasure of his will,

6 To the praise of the glory of his grace, wherein he hath made us accepted in the beloved.

7 In whom we have redemption through his blood, the forgiveness of sins, according to the riches of his grace;

8 Wherein he hath abounded toward us in all wisdom and prudence;

9 Having made known unto us the mystery of his will, according to his good pleasure which he hath purposed in himself:

10 That in the dispensation of the fulness of times he might gather together in one all things in Christ, both which are in heaven, and which are on earth; *even* in him:

11 In whom also we have obtained an inheritance, being predestinated according to the purpose of him who worketh all things after the counsel of his own will:

12 That we should be to the praise of his glory, who first trusted in Christ.

13 In whom ye also *trusted,* after that ye heard the word of truth, the gospel of your salvation: in whom also after that ye believed, ye were sealed with that holy Spirit of promise,

14 Which is the earnest of our inheritance until the redemption of the purchased possession, unto the praise of his glory.

NOTES

Chosen in Christ

Lesson Text: Ephesians 1:3-14

Related Scriptures: Acts 20:17-38; Romans 8:28-30;
II Thessalonians 2:13-17

TIME: A.D. 60　　　　　　　　　　　　　　　　　　PLACE: from Rome

GOLDEN TEXT—"[God] predestinated us unto the adoption of children by Jesus Christ to himself, according to the good pleasure of his will, to the praise of the glory of his grace" (Ephesians 1:5-6).

Lesson Exposition

GOD'S PAST ACTION—Eph. 1:3-6

He chose us (Eph. 1:3-4). Paul began by saying that God is to be blessed because He has blessed us with many spiritual blessings. God is worthy of adoration because He has conferred rich blessings on us and given many supernatural benefits. Paul described God as the Father of our Lord Jesus Christ and declared that our blessings come to us from heaven because of Christ. These benefits are nothing that we either earn or deserve; they are ours because of our relationship with God's Son, Jesus Christ.

Paul enumerated the spiritual blessings he had in mind, beginning with the truth that God chose us. God did this choosing in and through His Son, even before the physical Creation. This immediately raises a question that has been debated by theologians for centuries: How do we reconcile the truths presented in the Bible about God's sovereignty with mankind's free will? Ephesians 1:4 clearly states that God sovereignly chooses those who are to be His. Other Scriptures say God calls individuals to repent, but only some obey (Luke 7:30; 8:10; 13:34; 14:16-20).

"The Bible teaches that God is sovereign. The Bible also teaches that people can make choices. If you try to merge the two ideas, you will distort truth. If you try to remove all tension between the two, you will destroy one or the other of the truths, and possibly both. . . . They appear mutually exclusive to us because of a limitation either to our information or intelligence or both. The two truths are not mutually exclusive to God" (Anders, *Holman New Testament Commentary,* Broadman & Holman).

These two truths are an antinomy, a seeming contradiction between two equally valid truths that are held simultaneously. The best we can do is accept the fact that God's infinite wisdom does not communicate all He knows and understands to His finite creatures but that everything He does communicate is the truth.

He adopted us (Eph. 1:5-6). Part of God's choosing is that He predetermines that we should be placed into a family that is not naturally ours—namely, His own.

It is helpful to look at adoption in the Roman world in which Paul lived. The adopted person suddenly had all the rights of a legitimate son or daughter and was totally disconnected from his or her previous family relationships. Life was now new! All old debts and obligations were canceled as if they had never existed. The new position as an adopted child meant that the person enjoyed every privilege a natural-born child enjoyed. Of course, he was expected to live in a manner worthy of his new position.

God adopts into His family every person who receives Jesus Christ as personal Saviour. He gives them all the privileges of being His children. We do not have to grow into or earn those privileges; they are ours from the moment of salvation. Even more astounding is the fact that all of this is ours because He enjoys giving it to us! It is according to His pleasure and His will. It simply makes God happy to give us the joy of being His children. This should be an incentive to us to soberly accept our responsibilities along with our blessings.

The ultimate purpose of God's plan to choose us, save us, and adopt us is His own glory. We have nothing of which to feel proud; everything we have is because of the grace of God, and He is to receive all the glory. The word "beloved" in verse 6 refers to Christ. This means that we who are hopeless sinners are accepted and blessed not because we are worthy but because we are in Christ, the Beloved One of God.

OUR PRESENT REALITY—
Eph. 1:7-10

The riches of His grace (Eph. 1:7-8). Paul said we are redeemed from our sinful condition by the payment of Jesus' blood. As a result, we receive forgiveness of our sins. The Greek word translated "redemption" suggests a release from captivity. The purchase brings liberty!

This is an illustration of the fact that we are slaves to sin prior to our salvation. Since God created us, we are His, even though we became slaves to sin when Adam sinned. In His love and mercy, however, He paid the price to buy us back in order to set us free from the slavery of sin. That means we are free from the eternal penalty for sin (hell) and from the enslaving power of sin. Since we have within us the presence and power of the Holy Spirit, we do not have to live in sin. If we do live in sin, we show no fruits of redemption.

God has given all these blessings to us abundantly, according to the riches of His own grace. He also included the wisdom and understanding we need to comprehend it.

The mystery of His will (Eph. 1:9-10). Another thing God was pleased to show us is what Paul referred to as "the mystery of his will." A mystery is necessarily puzzling; it indicates there are obscure realities that await discovery. But when Paul spoke of a mystery, he was referring to spiritual truth that previously had been hidden from mankind but that now was being made known through revelation. In Romans 16:25-26, Paul spoke of the gospel message he was delivering as a mystery. It included the complete plan of salvation.

The mystery Paul spoke of in today's text is the truth that at the proper time, God would gather everything together under the authority of His Son. We know that after Jesus resurrected from the dead, He clearly stated, "All power is given unto me in heaven and in earth" (Matt. 28:18). The apostle Paul emphasized that Christ would reign until all His enemies are subdued (I Cor. 15:25). We will see a partial picture of this in the millennium, when Jesus will be the Ruler of earth from His throne in Jerusalem.

The complete fulfillment of this mystery, however, will come at the end of time and the beginning of eternity. Ever since sin entered God's universe, destruction and division have reigned.

Warren Wiersbe observed, "Sin is tearing everything apart, but in Christ, God will gather everything together in the culmination of the ages. We are a part of this great eternal program" (*The Bible Exposition Commentary,* Victor).

OUR FUTURE EXISTENCE—
Eph. 1:11-14

An inheritance (Eph. 1:11-12). From a first reading of these verses, we might get the impression that Paul was focusing mainly on the heavenly inheritance that we gain from our relationship with God through Jesus. But most likely, we should not limit this to heaven but rather include all the spiritual blessings we receive by being the children of God in Christ.

"The King James Version reads, 'In whom also we have obtained an inheritance,' but 'in whom also we were made an inheritance' is also a possible translation. Both are true and the one includes the other. In Christ we have a wonderful inheritance (I Peter 1:1-5) and in Christ we are an inheritance. We are valuable to Him. Think of the price God paid to purchase us and make us part of His inheritance! God the Son is the Father's love gift to us; and we are the Father's love gift to His Son" (Wiersbe).

To think that God, in the counsel of His own will, determined to make us His inheritance is indeed a humbling realization. Our being part of the heavenly crowd redounds to the praise of the glory of Jesus!

A guarantee (Eph. 1:13-14). The pronoun "you" ("ye") here designates the Gentiles, as opposed to the Jews who were the "we" in verses 11-12 (cf. 2:11-20). Three statements describe what had happened to them in their salvation. First, they "heard" (1:13). What was given to them was "the word of truth," that is, the good news of salvation through Jesus Christ, also called "the gospel."

Second, they "believed." It is not enough to hear about the possibility of salvation; there must be a response. It must be a response of belief in who Jesus is and what He has done to provide salvation. Third, they "were sealed." This sealing is a guarantee of our salvation. It was done by God with the Holy Spirit.

The word "earnest" means a pledge or a guarantee of something. Our ultimate salvation is described as "the redemption of the purchased possession" (vs. 14). The presence of the Holy Spirit within us is a pledge that one day we will indeed be in heaven in the presence of God.

—*Keith E. Eggert.*

QUESTIONS

1. What was the first spiritual blessing from God to His children that Paul mentioned?
2. What is an antinomy, and what two truths in Scripture fit this description?
3. What took place in Roman adoption, and how does it illustrate our adoption by God?
4. What is the meaning of "redemption," and what are the results of our having been redeemed?
5. What was God's motive in giving all these blessings to His own?
6. What is a biblical mystery?
7. What mystery did Paul mention in this week's text, and when will this mystery be fulfilled?
8. What does our inheritance in Christ include?
9. What is it that redounds to the praise of the glory of Jesus?
10. What does the presence of the Holy Spirit within us guarantee?

—*Keith E. Eggert.*

PRACTICAL POINTS

1. Our relationship with Christ is not only a daily experience but also an eternal one (Eph. 1:3-4).
2. We should never take for granted either God's acceptance of us or our relationship with Him (vss. 5-6).
3. Everything that God does for us is based on who and what He is, not on who we are (vss. 7-8).
4. Christ is the central figure of the ages, as well as of our lives (vss. 9-10).
5. We must always live in a manner worthy of our position as God's children and heirs (vss. 11-12).
6. God's gift of the Holy Spirit is just one of His many provisions for us (vss. 13-14).

—Anne Adams.

RESEARCH AND DISCUSSION

1. What does it mean practically to be "holy and without blame" (Eph. 1:4)? How does living that way help us serve God? Does that make us better than non-Christians? Discuss.
2. Some say our assurance of God's forgiveness means we might feel free to sin again because we know He will not reject us. How do you respond to this idea?
3. How do you determine God's will for your life? Is it difficult to know what it is?
4. In Bible times, someone's seal on a document verified the dependability of the one sealing it. How does this image help you understand God's "sealing" you in the Holy Spirit?

—Anne Adams.

Golden Text Illuminated

"[God] predestinated us unto the adoption of children by Jesus Christ to himself, according to the good pleasure of his will, to the praise of the glory of his grace" (Ephesians 1:5-6).

"According to the good pleasure of his will" tells us that the joy of God is found in His adoption of His children to Himself. By His power, His will then becomes the goal of all His people. When we look at the cross of Calvary, we can readily understand that there are no limits to God's care of those who need His healing grace. He showed the deepest passion for the healing of His people. The Father, in response to the willingness of His Son to bring healing, spoke His approval: "And there came a voice from heaven, saying, Thou art my beloved Son, in whom I am well pleased" (Mark 1:11).

When the Bible speaks of "the glory of his grace," it is telling us that God's glory is seen in His grace. It is His divine love that brings back the prodigal from the swine herds and affords true fellowship with the Father through Jesus Christ. He shows grace in order to "make known the riches of his glory on the vessels of mercy, which he had afore prepared unto glory, even us, whom he hath called, not of the Jews only, but also of the Gentiles" (Rom. 9:23-24).

How can we declare strongly enough that we owe everything to God's special gift of grace? The heart of every true believer is expressed in the phrase from Augustus Toplady's old hymn "Rock of Ages": "Simply to thy cross I cling."

—George A. Downes.

LESSON 6   JANUARY 7, 2024

Scripture Lesson Text

EPH. 2:1 And you *hath he quickened,* who were dead in trespasses and sins;

2 Wherein in time past ye walked according to the course of this world, according to the prince of the power of the air, the spirit that now worketh in the children of disobedience:

3 Among whom also we all had our conversation in times past in the lusts of our flesh, fulfilling the desires of the flesh and of the mind; and were by nature the children of wrath, even as others.

4 But God, who is rich in mercy, for his great love wherewith he loved us,

5 Even when we were dead in sins, hath quickened us together with Christ, (by grace ye are saved;)

6 And hath raised *us* up together, and made *us* sit together in heavenly *places* in Christ Jesus:

7 That in the ages to come he might shew the exceeding riches of his grace in *his* kindness toward us through Christ Jesus.

8 For by grace are ye saved through faith; and that not of yourselves: *it is* the gift of God:

9 Not of works, lest any man should boast.

10 For we are his workmanship, created in Christ Jesus unto good works, which God hath before ordained that we should walk in them.

NOTES

God's Workmanship

Lesson Text: Ephesians 2:1-10

Related Scriptures: Psalm 14:1-3; Ephesians 3:1-12; Titus 3:1-7

TIME: A.D. 60   PLACE: from Rome

GOLDEN TEXT—"For we are his workmanship, created in Christ Jesus unto good works, which God hath before ordained that we should walk in them" (Ephesians 2:10).

Lesson Exposition

DEAD!—Eph. 2:1-3

Sons of disobedience (Eph. 2:1-2). Paul used the word "dead" to describe those who have never experienced spiritual life. They are still physically alive, but without life in Christ, they are alienated from God. The only thing they are alive to is trespasses and sins. The Greek word for "trespasses" indicates a fall or a lapse. This can include unintentional errors and offenses. The Greek term for "sins" refers to a person failing to fulfill an obligation. It has often been interpreted as "missing the mark."

Those in this spiritually lifeless state slavishly follow "the course of this world" and are aligned with "the prince of the power of the air" (vs. 2). These facts point to an absence of light and life, reminding us again of spiritual death. The dark world of unbelievers is completely devoid of spiritual understanding, and this is the way Satan wants it. After all, "if our gospel be hid, it is hid to them that are lost: in whom the god of this world hath blinded the minds of them which believe not" (II Cor. 4:3-4).

The "prince of the power of the air" and "the spirit that now worketh in the children of disobedience" (Eph. 2:2) are probably one and the same, though some feel "spirit" refers back to the word "power," meaning "authority" (cf. 6:12). The "children of disobedience" are those who live in a state of unbelief.

Children of wrath (Eph. 2:3). As natural-born sinners, we were all under God's wrath. Mankind's rebellion against God can often be seen even in children when they are selfish and angry when they do not get their way. They commonly misbehave, are unkind, and lie. Since we are all Adam's descendants, we all inherited this nature. The word for "had our conversation" means "to conduct ourselves" or "to live." That includes everyone born, with no exceptions, so all of us began with the same need for deliverance from God's wrath.

In our sinful condition, our only motivation was to live according to the lusts of the flesh, that is, the sinful nature within us. The sinful lusts of our old nature were centered around satisfying fleshly desires, and this was our natural state. The pursuits that the unregenerate spend their lives on may actually be very enjoyable. They do not, however, provide genuine peace and satisfaction. We should note that there is a twofold description here. Some sinful actions come from cravings of our flesh and some from sinful thinking and motivations.

The biggest problem with being in this condition was that by our very nature we were objects of wrath. The wrath is God's, and the worst possible place to be is in opposition to an angry God! We were just like the rest of mankind, those who are still separated from Him.

The description Paul gave of those who are without Jesus Christ and living in their natural state is a portrait of hopelessness. Their only possible future is to suffer God's eternal wrath in hell. We have just read of the still-present worldly system in which we live. It is a system under the control of the devil, encouraging everyone to live in sinful indulgence. It centers around self to the exclusion of God, a situation that will never bring true joy.

ALIVE!—Eph. 2:4-7

Rich in mercy (Eph. 2:4-5). "But God"! Suddenly all the hopelessness melts away, for a solution has been provided! Verse 1 began by reminding us that we have been "quickened," that is, made alive. The shroud of spiritual death can indeed be removed in Christ; it need not drag us down to our earthly graves. The possibility of being alive is real because of God and what He has done for us.

In verse 4 God is described as being "rich in mercy" and having "great love" for us. Paul had already mentioned that we can have redemption through the blood of Jesus and the forgiveness of sins because of "the riches of his grace" (1:7). He would soon use the phrase "exceeding riches of his grace" to further express God's motivation (2:7). The Greek word *eleos* ("mercy" in vs. 4) indicates God's astonishing compassion and pity on wretched sinners who are helpless to change. Mercy is a primary motivation in Him saving undeserving foes.

"Love" translates *agapē*, which indicates preferential and self-sacrificing love. It is the kind of love that always seeks the highest good for the one loved.

This is the mercy and love that reached out to us when we were still dead in our sins. Once again we are told we have been made alive because of it, but now Paul adds that we are in union with Christ as a result. It has happened not only because of His mercy and love but also because of His grace. By that grace we have been saved and have passed from death to eternal life.

Rich in grace (Eph. 2:6-7). During Jesus' earthly lifetime, He raised only a few people physically from the dead. Since then, however, millions of us have been raised from death to life! While our bodies deteriorate and grow weak, our spiritual condition is actually more important than our physical. It is in the spiritual realm where we have been changed from being dead to being alive. The position we now have in Christ includes being made alive with Christ, being raised up with Him, and being seated with Him in the heavenly places (vss. 5-6). Our positional resurrection is described in the phrase "raised us up together."

Being alive in Christ assures us of a new life completely unlike the one we lived when we were spiritually dead. This strong contrast is stressed by the fact that we were raised to sit "together in heavenly places." We have been given a position of great importance in the realm where Christ sits at God's right hand. Because of our position with Christ, we have the power to defeat the "principalities" and "powers" we wrestle against (6:12).

Our spiritual resurrection points ahead to our physical resurrection, when we will be with Christ for all eternity. The way we live our new lives should be evidence of that and should be a testimony to all those around us of our relationship with Him.

All believers recognize to one degree or another their own unworthiness, since to come to Christ, one must seek His forgiveness. But we do not now fully know the extent of the grace of God. Throughout eternity, our understanding of it will grow ever deeper.

SAVED!—Eph. 2:8-10

Saved through faith (Eph. 2:8-9). All of this is a gift. This is the third mention of grace in this text, and it is another reminder that we have done nothing to earn the gift we receive.

God offers this gift of salvation and eternal life because of the "exceeding riches of his grace" mentioned in verse 7. Why would He do this for corrupt sinners? His gracious provision is motivated by "his great love wherewith he loved us" (vs. 4). It is a love greater than we can comprehend. Here is the crux of salvation: it is offered to us because of the grace of God and received by us in faith. Try to remember the phrase "by grace . . . through faith" when you need assurance of salvation. It tells us that redemption is not a cooperative effort with God.

The requirement of faith eliminates any basis for boasting. Salvation has absolutely nothing to do with what we contribute. It is available solely through faith. This makes Christianity absolutely unique among world religions. In every other religion, receiving heavenly rewards (or whatever a particular religion offers as a supreme goal) depends on a person's effort. Praise God for His grace!

Workmanship of God (Eph. 2:10). When it comes to our salvation, we have nothing in our own ability to give us a basis for boasting. Our salvation is not a masterpiece of our own doing; it is a masterpiece of God alone. The word for "workmanship" means "a product." We are saved by faith, not by hours of practice or training or anything else we can contribute. We are masterpieces of God and have done nothing but respond when it comes to our salvation. As God's works of art, therefore, we should be doing the good works He intends us to do.

All we are, all we have, and all that is ours for the future are because of Him and Him alone. Our primary goal through every day of life should be to live as He wants, to serve Him continually, and to enjoy His presence and fellowship.

—Keith E. Eggert.

QUESTIONS

1. What was Paul indicating when he called unbelievers dead?
2. What two terms describe the lives of people who are spiritually dead, and what do they mean?
3. How much spiritual light is there among unbelievers?
4. Why do we all have a sinful nature?
5. How does Ephesians 2:4 change the picture Paul was painting?
6. What three attributes of God are at work in making us alive in Christ?
7. What three things were done for us in Christ (vss. 5-6)?
8. What does our spiritual resurrection point to?
9. What did Paul say was the motivation behind God's gift?
10. Why are we devoid of reasons to boast about our salvation?

—Keith E. Eggert.

PRACTICAL POINTS

1. Thinking about the disobedience from which God has delivered us should humble us (Eph. 2:1-2).
2. Remembering our lives without Christ should make us thankful to be free from guilt and the fear of God's wrath (vs. 3).
3. God's love has given us new lives in Christ (vss. 4-5).
4. By releasing believers from their bondage to sin, God demonstrates His love to the world (vss. 6-7).
5. Through His grace, God has provided everything we need to believe and to be saved (vss. 8-9).
6. God has saved us to have a relationship with Him, to have freedom from condemnation, and to spread His love through good works (vs. 10).

—Cheryl Y. Powell.

RESEARCH AND DISCUSSION

1. At what times in your life have you felt separated from God? How has your relationship with God been restored after such times (cf. Titus 3:4-7)?
2. In what ways do some Christians behave as if they had earned salvation or were deserving of God's great love and kindness (cf. Eph. 2:8; Rom. 3:27-28; I Thess. 5:8-9)? How might their actions and attitudes affect the unsaved? How can the church address and correct those actions and attitudes?
3. What is the relationship between saving faith and good works (Eph. 2:9-10; cf. Jas. 2:14-26)?

—Cheryl Y. Powell.

Golden Text Illuminated

"For we are his workmanship, created in Christ Jesus unto good works, which God hath before ordained that we should walk in them" (Ephesians 2:10).

Our golden text is found at the conclusion of one of the Bible's most dramatic presentations of the powerful workings of God's grace in the lives of His people. Paul reminds us that we are created beings. Of course, God created the entire world and is the Author of every life. But here Paul is referring to a new creation that is presaging the new heavens and new earth. God's plan centers upon Christ being the Head of a redeemed people.

The golden text also gives us a needed reminder that God saves people for the purpose of becoming useful citizens of His kingdom. We were created for good works. Christ never thought in terms of a "salvation" that would not produce any fruit.

This call to good works should not seem burdensome. Having a worthwhile purpose in life is one of our primary needs, and no one could have any greater purpose than to serve God in ways that will last for eternity.

The golden text closes by declaring that God has already ordained the good works we are to perform. It is our responsibility to do the walking in good works that is referred to here. But the whole context of passage, being a grateful recounting of God's grace, should cause us not to recoil in anxiety from this assignment. We should instead rejoice in God's eternal plan, His sovereign empowerment, and His willingness to graciously include us in His work in this world.

—Stephen H. Barnhart.

LESSON 7  JANUARY 14, 2024

SCRIPTURE LESSON TEXT

EPH. 2:11 Wherefore remember, that ye *being* in time past Gentiles in the flesh, who are called Uncircumcision by that which is called the Circumcision in the flesh made by hands;

12 That at that time ye were without Christ, being aliens from the commonwealth of Israel, and strangers from the covenants of promise, having no hope, and without God in the world:

13 But now in Christ Jesus ye who sometimes were far off are made nigh by the blood of Christ.

14 For he is our peace, who hath made both one, and hath broken down the middle wall of partition *between us;*

15 Having abolished in his flesh the enmity, *even* the law of commandments *contained* in ordinances; for to make in himself of twain one new man, *so* making peace;

16 And that he might reconcile both unto God in one body by the cross, having slain the enmity thereby:

17 And came and preached peace to you which were afar off, and to them that were nigh.

18 For through him we both have access by one Spirit unto the Father.

19 Now therefore ye are no more strangers and foreigners, but fellowcitizens with the saints, and of the household of God;

20 And are built upon the foundation of the apostles and prophets, Jesus Christ himself being the chief corner *stone;*

21 In whom all the building fitly framed together groweth unto an holy temple in the Lord:

22 In whom ye also are builded together for an habitation of God through the Spirit.

NOTES

The Household of God

Lesson Text: Ephesians 2:11-22

Related Scriptures: John 10:14-18; Romans 5:1-11; Galatians 3:26-29

TIME: A.D. 60   PLACE: from Rome

GOLDEN TEXT—"In [Christ] all the building fitly framed together groweth unto an holy temple in the Lord" (Ephesians 2:21).

Lesson Exposition

A PROBLEM—Eph. 2:11-14

Alienated from Israel (Eph. 2:11-12). There were both Jews and Gentiles in the Ephesian church. Was there some friction between them that led Paul to focus on the Gentiles? Or was he simply answering questions that might have come up about the salvation of both groups?

When the Jews referred to the Gentiles as uncircumcised, they were speaking derogatorily. Circumcision had been the sign of the Jews' special relationship with God from the time of Abraham, and they were very proud of that relationship—even if they did not live according to God's commandments. It was a misplaced pride, because, as Paul explained in Romans 2:25-29, physical circumcision did not count for anything if their hearts were not right with God. In reality, circumcised Jews deserved God's wrath as much as Gentiles.

Paul then explained just how far away from God the Gentiles had been. Five truths are given. First, they were without Christ. Jesus came from a Jewish lineage to which the Gentiles had no claim whatsoever. They were outside God's family until He gave them the invitation to enter. Second, they were alienated from the Israelite nation, meaning they had no citizenship there. The Greek word translated "aliens" in Ephesians 2:12 means "to be estranged from" or "to be a nonparticipant." Gentiles had no part in this nation.

Third, they were strangers from the covenants of promise. Romans 9:4-5 explains this. Paul said the Jews were his kinsmen, "who are Israelites; to whom pertaineth the adoption, and the glory, and the covenants, and the giving of the law, and the service of God, and the promises; whose are the fathers, and of whom as concerning the flesh Christ came." Fourth, they had no hope. Fifth, they were without God in the world. Their condition was pitiable.

Brought near (Eph. 2:13-14). But there was good news for the Gentiles. Although they had been far off from access to a relationship with God in the past, God had now made a way for them to come near and have a relationship with Him. Paul said that it happened because of the blood of Jesus Christ. Why was the blood of Jesus so important?

Jesus' shedding of His blood on the cross made a way for both Jews and Gentiles to have a relationship with God. This reality greatly affected both groups, since they could now enjoy not only peace with God but also unity among both Jewish and Gentile believers. Before, they had been at odds; now there could be peace. That peace was actually Jesus Himself, because what He had done provided a way for the two different people groups to be unified and become one.

There had been a religious barrier separating the Jews and Gentiles, and this was evident even in the courts of the temple. There was a certain point beyond which the Gentiles were never allowed to go. A wall separated the two courts, with gates through which only Jews were allowed to enter. When Paul said in verse 14 that Christ "hath broken down the middle wall of partition between us," he was using a metaphor that had a literal counterpart in Jewish and Gentile experience.

A SOLUTION—Eph. 2:15-18

One new man (Eph. 2:15-16). The word "abolished" means "to completely destroy." The enmity that once existed between both Jews and Gentiles and God (through the law) is no longer in existence now that the wall of partition has been broken down. When a Jewish person receives Jesus as Saviour, he becomes part of the family of God; the same is true of any Gentile. In the family of God all distinctions between Jew and Gentile, male and female, slave and free are rendered unimportant (Gal. 3:28).

The Mosaic Law contained commands for numerous ritualistic ceremonies, feasts, and sacrifices. The Jews were the only people in the world of whom these rituals were required. Although the law itself did not create enmity between the Jews and the Gentiles, its requirements set the Jews apart from the Gentiles, thus creating an automatic division. Once Jesus fulfilled the requirements of the law, He created, through Himself, one entity instead of two. They were at peace, for Jesus had reconciled both to His Father by what He did on the cross. The enmity, as Paul stated, was put to death at that time.

To reconcile is to bring two or more parties back into a friendly relationship after there has been an estrangement. Because of the sacrifice of Jesus on the cross, payment was made for the sins of Jews and Gentiles alike. When individuals of either group receive Jesus as Saviour, they are back in a friendly and personal relationship with their Creator. Gentiles do not become Jews or vice versa; they both become Christians!

Mutual access (Eph. 2:17-18). Jesus came and preached peace to both groups of people. Those referred to as far off are the Gentiles (cf. vs. 13); they were not part of the relationship God had established with the Jews (vs. 12). The Jews are the ones described here as "them that were nigh" (vs. 17). Because of Jesus, Jews and Gentiles alike have access to His Father.

Verse 18 shows us that all three Persons of the Triune God are involved in this new relationship. Our access to God the Father is made possible by God the Son and is accomplished through God the Holy Spirit.

A RELATIONSHIP—Eph. 2:19-22

Fellow citizens (Eph. 2:19-20). "Strangers" are people who do not belong to a community. "Foreigners" are noncitizens living in the vicinity with limited rights and protections. This could refer to the Gentiles, who were now part of the family of God. Or it could refer to Jews and Gentiles alike, who were no longer strangers and foreigners to God's family. They were now fellow citizens in God's family. Race and nationality were irrelevant, because they were now equal members of the same family.

The change of relationship presented in verse 19 can also be viewed as pairs of contrasting opposites, with "strangers" being the opposite of "the household of God" and "foreigners" being the opposite of "fellow citizens." Because of Jesus, those who have received Him as Saviour are part of an eternal family whose Father is God. There is no longer any question about belonging. It is a family and household that has an incredibly strong foundation, so once we are part of it, we are safe and secure within it.

Paul wrote that our foundation consists of the apostles and prophets. Some commentators insist that the prophets here are exclusively New Testament ones (cf. Eph. 3:5; 4:11). Others interpret them as representing both Testaments (cf. II Pet. 3:2). Jesus Himself taught the disciples that the prophets spoke of Him (cf. Luke 24:27; John 5:39), although they did not fully reveal the mystery of the gospel.

This household (symbolized by a building) has Jesus as its cornerstone, the most important part of the foundation. He is the one who has made it possible for all of us to be included.

Holy temple (Eph. 2:21-22). The completed building, consisting of its Jewish and Gentile members, is now referred to as a holy temple for the Lord. Any building project consists of multiple pieces and parts and usually involves labor from many people. It is always enjoyable to see the many pieces getting put into place to form a whole. Eventually, the many parts and pieces become a single structure that God admires and dwells in.

"The stones are forming a living, spiritual temple to glorify the Lord. In the Old Testament the presence and glory of God inhabited a literal stone building. Now God dwells not in a stone building, but in the hearts of believers. Christ is the unifying factor that takes the separate stones and creates a temple. This temple is holy, set apart for God. In this temple God receives worship and praise. The hearts of believers is thus the basic worship place in God's kingdom on earth" (Anders, *Holman New Testament Commentary*, Broadman & Holman).

Being a citizen of a nation is legal and impersonal. Being a member of God's family is personal and warm. We who belong to Jesus Christ and are thus family members in God's household ought to enjoy the privilege of warm fellowship. Those who are without Christ in the world cannot begin to imagine the depth of relationships among God's children.

—Keith E. Eggert.

QUESTIONS

1. The Ephesian church included what two groups of people?
2. Why did the Jews look down on the Gentiles and speak negatively about them?
3. What five things described the Gentiles' distance from God?
4. How was that distance removed?
5. What changed in the relationship between the Jews and the Gentiles, and how did the temple illustrate their previous separation?
6. What was done to the enmity between Jews and Gentiles when Jesus made one new man out of two?
7. What does it mean for people to be reconciled to God?
8. What was preached that brought about mutual access to God for both Jews and Gentiles?
9. What changed for those described as strangers and foreigners?
10. What foundation led to the resulting holy temple for God?

—Keith E. Eggert.

PRACTICAL POINTS

1. Without Christ, we are spiritual strangers to God (Eph. 2:11-12).
2. Christ's blood allows sinners to approach God in faith (vs. 13).
3. Because Christ removed the barriers between God and us, as well as among all Christians, we all can serve Him together (vss. 14-16).
4. Sin kept sinners away from God, but in Christ He made peace and fellowship possible (vss. 17-18).
5. Believers in Christ are included in the holy communion of saints and in the family of God (vs. 19).
6. Christ is the foundation of our faith; He provides stability in an unstable world (vss. 20-22).

—Anne Adams.

RESEARCH AND DISCUSSION

1. Does your Christian faith set you apart from those in the world? How can it do so? Do they feel inadequate because you are a Christian and they are not? How do you respond if that is the case?
2. Why do some Christians reject other believers because they disagree on faith issues? Do they perhaps feel they must "separate"? Are all believers' disagreements resolved in Christ (Eph. 2:14)?
3. Specifically, how do we show God's love to others when we witness to them? How does saying the right thing help them believe?
4. What does it mean that the household of faith is built on the apostles and prophets (vs. 20)? How is Christ alike/different from them (vs. 21)?

—Anne Adams.

Golden Text Illuminated

"In [Christ] all the building fitly framed together groweth unto an holy temple in the Lord" (Ephesians 2:21).

When Jesus Christ came, He provided a new entrance to the holiness of God's presence by His eternal sacrifice. Not just a special priestly class but all true believers would have the right to enter. "Having therefore, brethren, boldness to enter into the holiest by the blood of Jesus, by a new and living way, which he hath consecrated for us, through the veil, that is to say, his flesh" (Heb. 10:19-20).

Now believers no longer need to go to a special location to worship God; He dwells within them. They are now the dwelling place of God Himself. "Know ye not that ye are the temple of God, and that the Spirit of God dwelleth in you?" (I Cor. 3:16).

This temple is "fitly framed"; that is, it is jointed together closely. No one would think of building a structure without a worthy foundation. The builder needs to be sure that the bricks are laid with care so that they will support the entire building. So God's temple is built and supported by His love and grace; it is not man-made.

Where will we find God? In the lives of His people. We are the witnesses for this generation. If anyone will look for Him, He will not be found in a particular building or in a faraway location. He will be found in the transformed lives of His people. There will be a difference between them and the world, and their lives will show the evidence of His presence.

—George A. Downes.

LESSON 8   JANUARY 21, 2024

Scripture Lesson Text

EPH. 4:1 I therefore, the prisoner of the Lord, beseech you that ye walk worthy of the vocation wherewith ye are called,

2 With all lowliness and meekness, with longsuffering, forbearing one another in love;

3 Endeavouring to keep the unity of the Spirit in the bond of peace.

4 *There is* **one body, and one Spirit, even as ye are called in one hope of your calling;**

5 One Lord, one faith, one baptism,

6 One God and Father of all, who *is* **above all, and through all, and in you all.**

7 But unto every one of us is given grace according to the measure of the gift of Christ.

8 Wherefore he saith, When he ascended up on high, he led captivity captive, and gave gifts unto men.

9 (Now that he ascended, what is it but that he also descended first into the lower parts of the earth?

10 He that descended is the same also that ascended up far above all heavens, that he might fill all things.)

11 And he gave some, apostles; and some, prophets; and some, evangelists; and some, pastors and teachers;

12 For the perfecting of the saints, for the work of the ministry, for the edifying of the body of Christ:

13 Till we all come in the unity of the faith, and of the knowledge of the Son of God, unto a perfect man, unto the measure of the stature of the fulness of Christ:

14 That we *henceforth* **be no more children, tossed to and fro, and carried about with every wind of doctrine, by the sleight of men,** *and* **cunning craftiness, whereby they lie in wait to deceive;**

15 But speaking the truth in love, may grow up into him in all things, which is the head, *even* Christ:

16 From whom the whole body fitly joined together and compacted by that which every joint supplieth, according to the effectual working in the measure of every part, maketh increase of the body unto the edifying of itself in love.

NOTES

A High Calling

Lesson Text: Ephesians 4:1-16

Related Scriptures: John 17:4-5; I Corinthians 12:12-31; I Peter 3:8-12

TIME: A.D. 60   PLACE: from Rome

GOLDEN TEXT—"I therefore, the prisoner of the Lord, beseech you that ye walk worthy of the vocation wherewith ye are called" (Ephesians 4:1).

Lesson Exposition

UNITY—Eph. 4:1-6

Worthy of your calling (Eph. 4:1-3). In the first three chapters of Ephesians, Paul laid out a doctrinal framework. He then wanted his readers to put this doctrinal teaching into daily living, so he began making application in 4:1: "I . . . beseech you that ye walk worthy of the vocation wherewith ye are called." His appeal came while he was under house arrest in Rome. He viewed himself as being there by the Lord's will, as seen in calling himself "the prisoner of the Lord."

The Greek word for "worthy" speaks of living appropriately. Such living is to be accomplished through three specific attitudes. "Lowliness" (vs. 2) refers to an attitude of humility, the opposite of pride.

The second attitude, "meekness," is a reference to a gentle spirit rather than one that is aggressive and harsh. Third, "longsuffering" is a spirit of patience that will enable believers to lovingly tolerate one another despite frustrations. As we allow the Holy Spirit to develop these attitudes in us, we will promote the unity and peaceful existence God wants among His own.

Hope of your calling (Eph. 4:4-6). As it is with any human body, so it is with the body of Christ—fractures cause nothing but pain and an inability to operate properly. The one body and one Spirit Paul mentioned are the first two of seven facets of the unity of the body of Christ. The next one is the common hope for eternal life with Him.

There is but one Lord for all of us. How can we not live in unity? He becomes our Saviour by the avenue of faith, and there is no other way, so we come by just one faith. That too is part of our unity. We also all share one baptism by the Spirit (I Cor. 12:13).

And over all is the one God and Father we share. Our unity is a result of the strong work of the Triune God.

GIFTS—Eph. 4:7-10

Grace given (Eph. 4:7-8). Paul quoted from Psalm 68:18, which portrays a military victor leading his captives home and giving gifts to his subjects. Many believe the captives here are those whom Christ set free.

The picture here is of Jesus, who won a great victory at the cross. He returned home, that is, ascended to heaven, victorious and with the ability to free all those who had been previously held captive by sin. Because of His victory, He was also able to give gifts to His people.

Victory won (Eph. 4:9-10). Verse 8 mentioned the ascension of Christ to the right hand of God in heaven following the resurrection (Acts 1:9-11; 2:29-35). This parenthetical statement argues that if Christ ascended, of necessity He had to have descended first.

There are varying opinions about what is meant in Ephesians 4:9. Some see it simply as the reverse of Jesus' ascension from earth to heaven.

There is a long history of viewing "the lower parts of the earth" as Hades (cf. Ps. 63:9). But Hades could simply refer to the place of the dead rather than to a place of torment.

The emphasis is on the contrast between His ascension and His descent. He ascended to a place of highest exaltation, "far above all heavens" (Eph. 4:10). He returned to His place of universal headship, to bestow gifts on whomever He wished.

BENEFITS—Eph. 4:11-16

Equipping and edifying (Eph. 4:11-12). The gifts mentioned here were given to the church so that it could have an effective ministry. These were leaders with Spirit-empowered abilities.

Four types of gifted church leaders are named here: apostles, prophets, evangelists, and pastor/teachers.

All these gifted men were meant to equip the believers to do the work of ministry and to build up the saints.

Unity and perfection (Eph. 4:13-14). The ultimate goal of the ministry of these gifted men and all those in the body of Christ is spiritual maturity.

For the "new man" (2:15), a growing faith and understanding of Jesus is of utmost importance if we are to grow spiritually and have an effective ministry to others. This will lead to spiritual maturity. In contrast, immature believers are easily influenced by false or inaccurate teachings. Those who deceive are described as using cunning craftiness and deceit (4:14). They lead others into instability rather than spiritual maturity. As a result, their followers are blown back and forth by the winds of confusing doctrine.

Growing and working (Eph. 4:15-16). Since Jesus Christ is the Head of the body of believers, it is important that we grow in our knowledge and understanding of Him. As we do, the body becomes more closely knit together, with each member becoming a significant part. It is from Christ, the Head, that the body gets its capacity for continual growth.

—Keith E. Eggert.

QUESTIONS

1. What did Paul begin to do in Ephesians 4?
2. How did Paul say he wanted believers to live, and what three attitudes accomplish this?
3. What similar effect is true for the body of Christ and a human body?
4. What is the one way to receive Christ?
5. What truth does the imagery of Christ leading captives home portray?
6. What contrast did Paul emphasize in describing where Jesus went?
7. What gifted men did Jesus give to the church to edify it?
8. What was the ultimate goal of the ministry of these men?
9. How are spiritually immature believers affected by false teaching?
10. How does one believer's growth in Christ affect the body?

—Keith E. Eggert.

PRACTICAL POINTS

1. It is not a burden but a blessing and a privilege for us to follow God (Eph. 4:1-3).
2. Being one in Christ means that our common purpose and goal should be to glorify God (vss. 4-6).
3. With God's grace, we are free from the worry that we cannot earn what He gives us (vss. 7-8).
4. The gifts of grace we receive come because of Christ's victory (vss. 9-13).
5. False doctrine and deceitful teaching do not sway those who become mature in their faith (vs. 14).
6. Each spiritual gift is designed to harmonize perfectly with the gifts of others in the church (vss. 15-16).
—Anne Adams.

RESEARCH AND DISCUSSION

1. How does it encourage church unity when Christians love and respect each other (Eph. 4:1-3)?
2. What is/are your spiritual gift(s)? How do you use it? How can you use it better?
3. Some believe that the more obvious spiritual gifts are more important because they are more impressive. How do you respond to this idea? Do the more obvious gifts actually glorify God more than the "behind the scenes" type? Why or why not?
4. How can you and others in your church best use your spiritual gifts together for God? Do some people have unrecognized gifts you can encourage them to develop?
—Anne Adams.

Golden Text Illuminated

"I therefore, the prisoner of the Lord, beseech you that ye walk worthy of the vocation wherewith ye are called" (Ephesians 4:1).

The opening words of the golden text may jolt us a bit. Paul calls himself a "prisoner of the Lord." He knew himself to be the Lord's bond servant (cf. Rom. 1:1), and he was grateful for that privilege.

Paul was, of course, literally a prisoner as he wrote this letter. Ephesians is one of the Prison Epistles. He was under house arrest in Rome. He was in no way bitter about this, though. He recognized himself to be principally the Lord's—not the Romans'—prisoner. This helped him bear up under hardship.

The apostle took pains to press upon ("beseech") his readers regarding the importance of living their lives in a way that honored the God they served. The context indicates that Paul was especially concerned that the Ephesian believers recognize the significance of belonging to Christ's church.

The church, uniting Jew and Gentile in the body of Christ, was the mystery at the heart of God's plan for centuries. We are to walk worthy of our vocation of service, our God-appointed calling, in Christ's church.

First, we should fully embrace the spiritual gift or gifts that Christ blesses us with. Second, we are to live holy lives (4:17—5:20). Third, we are to honor God through our families (5:21—6:9).

Christian vocation is not just for a special group of "full-time," dedicated workers. Every believer's vocation is to daily commit every area of life to Christ and serve His church. May we be ever faithful to that calling.

—Stephen H. Barnhart.

LESSON 9 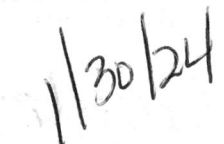 JANUARY 28, 2024

Scripture Lesson Text

EPH. 5:21 Submitting yourselves one to another in the fear of God.

22 Wives, submit yourselves unto your own husbands, as unto the Lord.

23 For the husband is the head of the wife, even as Christ is the head of the church: and he is the saviour of the body.

24 Therefore as the church is subject unto Christ, so *let* **the wives** *be* **to their own husbands in every thing.**

25 Husbands, love your wives, even as Christ also loved the church, and gave himself for it;

26 That he might sanctify and cleanse it with the washing of water by the word,

27 That he might present it to himself a glorious church, not having spot, or wrinkle, or any such thing; but that it should be holy and without blemish.

28 So ought men to love their wives as their own bodies. He that loveth his wife loveth himself.

29 For no man ever yet hated his own flesh; but nourisheth and cherisheth it, even as the Lord the church:

30 For we are members of his body, of his flesh, and of his bones.

31 For this cause shall a man leave his father and mother, and shall be joined unto his wife, and they two shall be one flesh.

32 This is a great mystery: but I speak concerning Christ and the church.

33 Nevertheless let every one of you in particular so love his wife even as himself; and the wife *see* that she reverence *her* husband.

6:1 Children, obey your parents in the Lord: for this is right.

2 Honour thy father and mother; (which is the first commandment with promise;)

3 That it may be well with thee, and thou mayest live long on the earth.

4 And, ye fathers, provoke not your children to wrath: but bring them up in the nurture and admonition of the Lord.

NOTES

God-Honoring Families

Lesson Text: Ephesians 5:21—6:4

Related Scriptures: Colossians 3:18-21; I Peter 3:1-7

TIME: A.D. 60　　　　　　　　　　　　　　PLACE: from Rome

GOLDEN TEXT—"[Submit] yourselves one to another in the fear of God" (Ephesians 5:21).

Lesson Exposition

SUBMISSION—Eph. 5:21-24

A biblical principle (Eph. 5:21). This verse is somewhat transitional in nature, completing the thoughts about the evidences of being Spirit-filled and at the same time introducing an important principle that is necessary for good human relationships. The teaching of mutual submission is important, partly because some in authority distort teachings about authority.

Wives must submit to their husbands, but husbands should also submit to their wives as they would to any other believer. Children must submit to parents, but parents should be humble enough to truly listen and give due consideration to their children's opinions and complaints. Workers must submit to employers, but Christian employers should be attentive to the concerns and needs of their employees.

A biblical authority (Eph. 5:22-24). It is regrettable that these verses trigger immediate negative reactions from many readers. The emphasis is laid on the wife's respect for the authority God has placed over her, not on the husband's respectability. A wife's submission to her husband is to be parallel to the husband's submission to Christ. In this way, her submission to her husband is also a submission to the Lord, whom both should desire to please. Paul said that just as Christ is the Head over the church, so the husband is the head over his wife. It is a matter of leadership, not dictatorial authority.

LOVE—Eph. 5:25-33

A sanctifying love (Eph. 5:25-27). When a husband loves his wife in the same way that Christ loves His church, the wife never needs to fear being in submission. A husband with this kind of love for his wife will dedicate himself to her physical, mental, emotional, and spiritual well-being. If he fulfills his role in this way, it is easier for her to fulfill hers.

A selfless love (Eph. 5:28-29). The kind of love Paul now describes is that which any person exhibits for his or her own body. Our bodies are never perfect, but we care about them and do the best we can to keep them healthy and operative. We give ourselves nourishing food, practice habits of cleanliness, and hopefully get sufficient exercise, all in order to keep our bodies healthy. This is natural and proper, but so is a husband giving loving care to his wife. For a man to neglect or abuse his wife is abnormal and unreasonable.

A separated love (Eph. 5:30-31). Ephesians 4:25 tells us that "we are members one of another," which is now explained as members of the body of Jesus Christ.

Since the body of Christ is one even though it has multitudes of members, the husband/wife relationship should be easily understood for what God wants it to be. As Christ cares for every member of His body, so the husband should care for his wife. This relationship was established at Creation and is referred to here in a quote of Genesis 2:24. The union of marriage is intimate and unbreakable.

A symbolic love (Eph. 5:32-33). Here is a mystery, that is, a truth that had previously been hidden from mankind. And according to Paul, this one is big ("a great mystery")! In other words, he was about to set forth a profound truth about marriage. As imperfect as a human marriage is, it is a portrait of the relationship between Christ and His church. This brings a perspective to the marriage relationship that those who are outside of God's family will never understand—and one that too many believers ignore as well.

OBEDIENCE—Eph. 6:1-4

A command with promise (Eph. 6:1-3). In Paul's day, children were not considered very important people. It is quite unusual, therefore, that he would specifically address them in this letter.

Just as wives are told to be submissive to husbands as a way to honor the Lord, so children are to be obedient to their parents for the same reason. The fact that this obedience is "in the Lord" (vs. 1) does not mean they were to obey only if their parents were believers.

The promise of long life is a general one and not intended to be claimed in every situation. But obedient children do have a better prospect of living safely and longer.

A command with instruction (Eph. 6:4). It is one thing to discipline children but quite another to exasperate them with unreasonable demands and degrading words.

Fathers must not drive them away from the Lord by discouraging or hurting them.

In fact, the instruction that accompanies this command is that fathers should train their children in the things of the Lord. A father's primary purpose should be to see his children become adults who love and obey God.

—Keith E. Eggert

QUESTIONS

1. How is Ephesians 5:21 a transitional verse, and what two subjects does it connect?
2. How can there be mutual submission in the family and in the work setting?
3. Why should women not react negatively to the command to submit to their husbands?
4. What truth illustrates the husband's role as head of the family?
5. How can a husband make it easier for his wife to exercise submission?
6. How did Paul show that it is natural for a man to love his wife?
7. How does being members of the body of Christ relate to how we should behave in a marriage?
8. What Old Testament verse clearly establishes marital permanence?
9. What is the mystery in verse 32?
10. What should a father's primary purpose be for his children?

—Keith E. Eggert

PRACTICAL POINTS

1. Submitting to other Christians demonstrates Christlike humility (Eph. 5:21).
2. When we surrender to the Lord, we trust Him to make the right decisions for us (vss. 22-24).
3. Christ's love for the church means He has a personal interest in every believer (vss. 25-29).
4. Unity in marriage, as in the Christian life, glorifies God (vss. 30-33).
5. Obeying parents helps children understand how they should follow God (6:1-3).
6. A parent's love for a child should reflect Christ's love for His church (vs. 4).

—Anne Adams.

RESEARCH AND DISCUSSION

1. If a woman's husband is abusive, does that mean she should still submit to him in everything? Is she justified in submitting in some areas and not in others?
2. How should a person respond to a spouse who demeans him or her? What if one is a Christian and the other is not? If you know someone in that situation, how can you help that person?
3. Is it possible to love one's spouse without respecting him or her? What can be done to establish both love and respect?
4. How does a single parent provide the love and encouragement that would normally come from the absent parent? How can the church help such parents? Discuss.

—Anne Adams.

Golden Text Illuminated

"[Submit] yourselves one to another in the fear of God" (Ephesians 5:21).

In the New Testament, God confirmed the idea of authority for the home and life in general. Can we imagine a company where there is no supervision and each employee does whatever he feels like doing regardless of what the outcome might be? Of course not! Someone must be in charge to make sure the product is produced correctly.

The major difference between the behavior of the world and that of the Christian is that love is the foundation of the order of authority in the Christian community. "Husbands, love your wives, even as Christ also loved the church, and gave himself for it" (vs. 25). The model set before us is Christ's love and what He did. The Christian must walk in the same spirit that Christ walked. His love was authentic, and we need to have the kind of obedience that comes from the heart.

God is not honored by confusion. He is a God of orderliness, and His creation bears this out. Everything in nature speaks of order, and the witness of God is present in what He has made. All the heavens show His handiwork. When we look at them, we should stand in awe, even as David did. "When I consider thy heavens, the work of thy fingers, the moon and the stars, which thou hast ordained; what is man, that thou art mindful of him? and the son of man, that thou visitest him?" (Ps. 8:3-4).

—George A. Downes.

LESSON 10   2/6/24   FEBRUARY 4, 2024

SCRIPTURE LESSON TEXT

EPH. 6:10 Finally, my brethren, be strong in the Lord, and in the power of his might.

11 Put on the whole armour of God, that ye may be able to stand against the wiles of the devil.

12 For we wrestle not against flesh and blood, but against principalities, against powers, against the rulers of the darkness of this world, against spiritual wickedness in high *places.*

13 Wherefore take unto you the whole armour of God, that ye may be able to withstand in the evil day, and having done all, to stand.

14 Stand therefore, having your loins girt about with truth, and having on the breastplate of righteousness;

15 And your feet shod with the preparation of the gospel of peace;

16 Above all, taking the shield of faith, wherewith ye shall be able to quench all the fiery darts of the wicked.

17 And take the helmet of salvation, and the sword of the Spirit, which is the word of God:

18 Praying always with all prayer and supplication in the Spirit, and watching thereunto with all perseverance and supplication for all saints;

19 And for me, that utterance may be given unto me, that I may open my mouth boldly, to make known the mystery of the gospel,

20 For which I am an ambassador in bonds: that therein I may speak boldly, as I ought to speak.

21 But that ye also may know my affairs, *and* how I do, Tychicus, a beloved brother and faithful minister in the Lord, shall make known to you all things:

22 Whom I have sent unto you for the same purpose, that ye might know our affairs, and *that* he might comfort your hearts.

23 Peace *be* to the brethren, and love with faith, from God the Father and the Lord Jesus Christ.

24 Grace *be* with all them that love our Lord Jesus Christ in sincerity. Amen.

NOTES

Spiritual Armor

Lesson Text: Ephesians 6:10-24

Related Scriptures: Romans 8:26-27; II Corinthians 10:1-5; I Peter 5:6-11

TIME: A.D. 60   PLACE: from Rome

GOLDEN TEXT—"Put on the whole armour of God, that ye may be able to stand against the wiles of the devil" (Ephesians 6:11).

Lesson Exposition

POWER FOR THE STRUGGLE—Eph. 6:10-12

God's strength (Eph. 6:10). In their own power and wisdom, Christians are no match for Satan. For this reason, Paul encouraged the Ephesians by reminding them of their source of strength. The almighty God is the infinite source of power for His people. Satan is no match for Him or for people empowered by His might.

God's armor (Eph. 6:11). Christians need spiritual armor. This comes from God Himself. In fact, some of the pieces of armor Paul listed seem to be taken directly from Isaiah's description of the divine warrior (59:17). God's armor protects His people from the schemes of the devil.

God's battle (Eph. 6:12). The Bible teaches about the conflict between God and Satan (cf. Rev. 12:7-9). By attacking God's people and encouraging sin, Satan endeavors to subvert God's plan. Christians, therefore, are a particular target of the devil.

Against believers Satan throws the full weight of his forces, including all the various ranks of evil angels. It is no wonder that Christians need God's armor.

PROVISION FOR THE STRUGGLE—Eph. 6:13-17

Purpose for the armor (Eph. 6:13). God's spiritual armor is essential when the days become difficult. Christians can keep fighting rather than give up. It is God's purpose that His armor will equip believers to stand victorious in His power.

Protection by the armor (Eph. 6:14). Paul here listed the pieces of armor. The belt protected the loins and kept the breastplate straight. The belt of truth may refer both to the integrity of the Christian and to the truth of God's Word. The point? Unswerving commitment to God's Word and God's way is crucial if the believer is to stand against the attacks of Satan.

The breastplate provided protection for organs such as the heart and the lungs. The breastplate for the Christian is righteousness.

Righteousness probably refers to the righteousness of God, which is imputed to Christians by virtue of the merits of Christ. Those who stand in the righteousness of Christ are protected in the battle.

Preparation of the armor (Eph. 6:15). Christian soldiers in battle have the secure footing of the good news that Christ's death has provided peace with God. Because peace with God comes through what Christ did, they can stand firmly.

Potential of the armor (Eph. 6:16). After putting on his body armor, the soldier took up his shield. God has given Christians the shield of faith. By faith, Christians can proceed steadfastly in full confidence the Lord will keep His promises.

Power of the armor (Eph. 6:17). The helmet was designed to withstand severe blows to the head. The helmet of salvation is to be received. Salvation is received from God, not gained by human effort.

Last of all, Paul spoke of the sword of the Spirit, the Word of God. Christ used the Word of God to counter the temptations of Satan (Matt. 4:1-11). Christians must use the Bible as they confront the evil one.

The sword was both a defensive and an offensive weapon. The Word of God can protect against doubt, fear, and fatigue. The Bible also enables Christians to advance God's work (II Cor. 10:4-5).

PRAYER FOR THE STRUGGLE— Eph. 6:18-24

Prayer for one another (Eph. 6:18). Paul appealed to the Ephesians to pray for one another. Christians should pray that all believers will be able to stand in the struggle. Without prayer they will most likely stumble.

Prayer for Paul (Eph. 6:19-20). After Paul instructed the Ephesians to pray for one another, he asked them also to pray for him. He requested prayer that he would be able to speak boldly when he was given the occasion to declare his commitment to Christ. Paul knew that he would have a golden opportunity to make the gospel known to Caesar.

Paul used a striking picture to describe his circumstances. As a prisoner, he was chained. At the same time, he was an ambassador of Christ sent on God's official business.

Prospect of Tychicus (Eph. 6:21-22). As Paul concluded his letter, he commended to the Ephesians Tychicus, the man who was bearing the epistle to them. Tychicus would be able to share with them more details of Paul's condition.

Peace to the Ephesians (Eph. 6:23-24). In his final words Paul blessed the Ephesians by calling for God's peace, love, and grace to be with them.

—*Daniel J. Estes.*

QUESTIONS

1. What is the source of strength for Christians as they face spiritual conflicts?
2. From where did Paul derive his picture of the Christian's armor?
3. How are the struggles of individual Christians related to the conflict between God and Satan?
4. What is the ultimate purpose for the Christian's armor?
5. Why is the belt of truth essential for spiritual victory?
6. How does the righteousness of Christ serve as a breastplate for the Christian soldier?
7. How does the Christian soldier maintain secure footing?
8. How does faith enable Christians to advance the cause of Christ in the face of opposition?
9. How is the Word of God both a defensive and offensive weapon?
10. How did Paul demonstrate the necessity of mutual prayer?

—*Daniel J. Estes.*

PRACTICAL POINTS

1. Apart from God's help, we are no match for Satan (Eph. 6:10-11).
2. Our greatest adversary is not the person who opposes the gospel but the spiritual power that inspires that opposition (vs. 12).
3. We can resist Satan's temptations only if we are solidly grounded in the truth and are living out that truth in our lives (vss. 13-15).
4. A living faith coupled with a knowledge of God's Word is our best defense against the errors Satan promotes (vss. 16-17).
5. Continual prayer is necessary if the gospel is to go forth boldly and effectively (vss. 18-20).
6. The encouragement of fellow believers is a ministry in which we all should participate (vss. 21-22).
7. Real peace is a blessing that comes only from God (vss. 23-24).

—Jarl K. Waggoner.

RESEARCH AND DISCUSSION

1. What makes a Christian spiritually strong (Eph. 6:10)?
2. Why is it important to know our enemy (vs. 12)? How can we be prepared without being paranoid?
3. What roles do the various pieces of spiritual armor play in our daily struggles (vss. 14-17)?
4. How can we fulfill the scriptural ideal of "praying always" (Eph. 6:18; cf. I Thess. 5:17)?
5. What specific steps could your church take to improve its ministry of prayer?

—Jarl K. Waggoner.

Golden Text Illuminated

"Put on the whole armour of God, that ye may be able to stand against the wiles of the devil" (Ephesians 6:11).

Whether we like it or not, every Christian is involved in spiritual warfare. As believers, we are not called to a life of passivity. We do not wear armor for a pleasant stroll in the park.

The golden text reminds us that our chief enemy in our spiritual warfare is "the devil," Satan himself. As the following verse tells us, we are wrestling against powerful spiritual foes.

Paul told Timothy he had kept the faith through his fight (II Tim. 4:7), and Ephesians 6:16 says we need the shield of faith to stand against Satan's attacks. Faith is the key.

Satan wants to destroy our faith, our walk with God. The Lord has ordained that He will keep His people safe (John 6:39; 17:2-3; Phil. 1:6). We have nothing to fear. He will preserve His people. But it is nevertheless true that He has ordained that believers make use of the means of warfare that He provides.

The battle we are in is so serious that we must not neglect any of the provisions the Lord supplies. We must utilize the *whole* armor. And we must not depend on the world's weapons (cf. II Cor. 10:3-4). It is the armor of God that we need.

One reason we need all the resources God provides is that our enemy is crafty. We can see his craftiness in Eden, where he was successful in bringing about man's fall, and even in his failed efforts to tempt our sinless Lord.

Yes, we are engaged in spiritual warfare. In His great grace, God has provided all we need to defeat our enemy.

—Stephen H. Barnhart.

Scripture Lesson Text

COL. 1:15 Who is the image of the invisible God, the firstborn of every creature:

16 For by him were all things created, that are in heaven, and that are in earth, visible and invisible, whether *they be* **thrones, or dominions, or principalities, or powers: all things were created by him, and for him:**

17 And he is before all things, and by him all things consist.

18 And he is the head of the body, the church: who is the beginning, the firstborn from the dead; that in all *things* **he might have the preeminence.**

19 For it pleased *the Father* that in him should all fulness dwell;

20 And, having made peace through the blood of his cross, by him to reconcile all things unto himself; by him, *I say,* **whether** *they be* **things in earth, or things in heaven.**

21 And you, that were sometime alienated and enemies in *your* mind by wicked works, yet now hath he reconciled

22 In the body of his flesh through death, to present you holy and unblameable and unreproveable in his sight:

23 If ye continue in the faith grounded and settled, and *be* not moved away from the hope of the gospel, which ye have heard, *and* which was preached to every creature which is under heaven; whereof I Paul am made a minister;

24 Who now rejoice in my sufferings for you, and fill up that which is behind of the afflictions of Christ in my flesh for his body's sake, which is the church:

25 Whereof I am made a minister, according to the dispensation of God which is given to me for you, to fulfil the word of God;

26 *Even* **the mystery which hath been hid from ages and from generations, but now is made manifest to his saints:**

27 To whom God would make known what *is* the riches of the glory of this mystery among the Gentiles; which is Christ in you, the hope of glory:

28 Whom we preach, warning every man, and teaching every man in all wisdom; that we may present every man perfect in Christ Jesus.

NOTES

The Supremacy of Christ

Lesson Text: Colossians 1:15-28

Related Scriptures: John 1:15-18; II Corinthians 5:17-21; Revelation 5:1-14

TIME: A.D. 60 PLACE: from Rome

GOLDEN TEXT—"It pleased the Father that in [Christ] should all fulness dwell" (Colossians 1:19).

Lesson Exposition

CHRIST, THE CREATOR OF THE WORLD—Col. 1:15-17

The Firstborn of all creation (Col. 1:15). Because Christ is deity, He is the Firstborn of every creature in the universe. The term "firstborn" may sound as though Christ were an exalted but created being. If that were the case, He would be a creature inferior to God instead of being truly divine. In reality, the biblical notion of the "firstborn" speaks of one who has the legal privilege of inheritance and ownership. As the eternal Son of God, Christ has authority over everything that has been created. He is the Lord of the universe, the Sovereign of the world, the one who merits all worship and adoration.

The Creator of all things (Col. 1:16). Paul stated that all things were created by Christ. The New Testament teaches clearly that Jesus was the active Agent in creating the world. All things that can be seen and the things that are invisible came into existence by His activity. Even the various ranks of angels were made by Him.

All things were made by Him, and all things have a definite purpose in His plan. Consequently, all creation should acknowledge Him as Lord.

The Sustainer of all things (Col. 1:17). Christ existed before Creation, and all things owe their existence to Him. Moreover, apart from Christ's continuing work in sustaining the world, all things would fall apart. Christ maintains the universe He called into being. He is the source of all life, and He sustains it all.

CHRIST, THE HEAD OF THE CHURCH—Col. 1:18-23

The preeminent position (Col. 1:18). Paul frequently used the figure of a human body to speak of the church. Christ is the Head of the body. Just as Christ is preeminent over all the world that He created, so He is preeminent in the church He has redeemed.

The peace of reconciliation (Col. 1:19-20). One of the false teachings in Colossae alleged that Christ was a created being.

Paul rejected that false notion by stating that Christ is the divine Creator. He is the one who also died and rose again to become the Head of the church. That opened up the door to reconciliation between a holy God and unholy humans. Those who accept Christ's death for them are accepted by God on the merits of Christ's sacrifice. Through

Christ, God reconciles all things to Himself, both things in earth and things in heaven. In the end Christ will subdue even Satan (Rev. 20:10). There will be a new heaven and a new earth in which God rules in perfect righteousness.

The purifying death (Col. 1:21-22). The Colossian Christians' sin and unbelief had made them the enemies of God. Their wicked deeds were opposed to God's righteous standards.

Christ, however, had wonderfully transformed the believers' lives. In their sinful condition, the Colossians had been unwilling and unable to please God. Through Christ's death on the cross, the Colossian Christians had been personally reconciled to God.

Christ can present Christians as holy, unblemished, and beyond accusation in God's sight. Even though Christians do sin at times, in Christ they can stand before a holy God. Moreover, through the process of sanctification, Christ is continuing to refine the lives of His people.

The priority of faith (Col. 1:23). There is always the danger that people who profess salvation can be led astray into error. Paul urged the Colossians to continue in their faith in Christ. In so doing they would prove that they had been genuinely reconciled to God.

Paul urged the believers not to be moved from their hope in Christ. This constituted the central focus of Paul's ministry.

CHRIST, THE HOPE OF GLORY—
Col. 1:24-28

Paul's suffering for Christ (Col. 1:24). Paul suffered as he labored to bring the gospel to people. Just as Christ suffered during His earthly ministry, so Paul, as a member of Christ's body, continued Christ's suffering as he preached the gospel to the world.

Paul's stewardship from Christ (Col. 1:25-26). As a minister of the gospel, Paul had received a specific commission and responsibility from God. Paul did not invent his message, and he did not design his own course of action. God gave him the task of revealing the mystery of the gospel that had been hidden in times past.

Paul's statement about Christ (Col. 1:27-28). Wherever Paul went, he had a single goal. His desire was to bring people to spiritual maturity in Christ. His preaching entailed positive instruction to Christians so that they could reach their spiritual potential.

—*Daniel J. Estes.*

QUESTIONS

1. In what sense is Christ the Firstborn of every creature?
2. How extensive was Christ's creative activity?
3. How is Christ essential to the continuance of the world that He created?
4. What relationship does Christ have to the church?
5. By what means does God reconcile all things to Himself?
6. How had Christ already transformed the lives of the Colossians from what they had been before?
7. Why did Paul urge the Colossians to continue in the faith?
8. In what way did Paul fill up the afflictions of Christ through his own sufferings?
9. What responsibility did God give Paul?
10. What was the ultimate goal of Paul's ministry?

—*Daniel J. Estes.*

PRACTICAL POINTS

1. We have been created by Christ and for Him; thus, we fulfill our purpose for existence when we bring glory to Him (Col. 1:15-17).
2. As members of Christ's body, we are to look to Him for spiritual growth and guidance (vss. 18-19).
3. To fully appreciate God's work in our lives, we need to remind ourselves of the depths from which He has lifted us (vss. 20-21).
4. We experience assurance of Christ's saving and preserving work in our lives as we continue in sound doctrine and living faith (vss. 22-23).
5. We must never allow suffering to deter us from declaring God's Word; our trials may be sent upon us to benefit others (vss. 24-25).
6. We should show by our lives and words that the only sure basis for future hope is in knowing Christ as personal Saviour (vss. 26-28).

—Jarl K. Waggoner.

RESEARCH AND DISCUSSION

1. What verses from our lesson text would you use to try to convince someone of Christ's deity?
2. What implications does Christ's being the "head of the... church" (Col. 1:18) have for a local congregation?
3. How would you answer someone who claims that verse 20 teaches that all people will be saved?
4. What in verses 23-28 illustrates the preeminence of Christ (cf. vs. 18) in Paul's life and ministry?
5. In what sense does this passage summarize our responsibilities?

—Jarl K. Waggoner.

Golden Text Illuminated

"It pleased the Father that in [Christ] should all fulness dwell" (Colossians 1:19).

What do you think of Jesus? Who do you think He really was?

How you answer these questions is very important; your answer will determine how you respond to what Scripture reveals about Him.

Consider the opening words of Hebrews: "God, who at sundry times and in divers manners spake in time past unto the fathers by the prophets, hath in these last days spoken unto us by his Son, whom he hath appointed heir of all things, by whom also he made the worlds; who being the brightness of his glory, and the express image of his person, and upholding all things by the word of his power" (Heb. 1:1-3).

Jesus is the last word from God. Jesus is the full and complete manifestation of God. When we see and hear Christ in Scripture, we are in fact viewing and listening to God.

Jesus Himself made the same assertion: "He that hath seen me hath seen the Father" (John 14:9).

Why did Jesus come to the earth to make God known? John gave this answer: Christ "came unto his own, and his own received him not. But as many as received him, to them gave he power to become the sons of God, even to them that believe on his name" (John 1:11-12).

Jesus did not come to earth so that He could be known as a great prophet or moral teacher. He did not come to merely be our example. He came to make it possible for us to know God Himself.

—James R. Gordon.

LESSON 12   FEBRUARY 18, 2024

Scripture Lesson Text

COL. 2:6 As ye have therefore received Christ Jesus the Lord, *so* walk ye in him:

7 Rooted and built up in him, and stablished in the faith, as ye have been taught, abounding therein with thanksgiving.

8 Beware lest any man spoil you through philosophy and vain deceit, after the tradition of men, after the rudiments of the world, and not after Christ.

9 For in him dwelleth all the fulness of the Godhead bodily.

10 And ye are complete in him, which is the head of all principality and power:

11 In whom also ye are circumcised with the circumcision made without hands, in putting off the body of the sins of the flesh by the circumcision of Christ:

12 Buried with him in baptism, wherein also ye are risen with *him* through the faith of the operation of God, who hath raised him from the dead.

13 And you, being dead in your sins and the uncircumcision of your flesh, hath he quickened together with him, having forgiven you all trespasses;

14 Blotting out the handwriting of ordinances that was against us, which was contrary to us, and took it out of the way, nailing it to his cross;

15 *And* having spoiled principalities and powers, he made a shew of them openly, triumphing over them in it.

16 Let no man therefore judge you in meat, or in drink, or in respect of an holyday, or of the new moon, or of the sabbath *days:*

17 Which are a shadow of things to come; but the body *is* of Christ.

18 Let no man beguile you of your reward in a voluntary humility and worshipping of angels, intruding into those things which he hath not seen, vainly puffed up by his fleshly mind,

19 And not holding the Head, from which all the body by joints and bands having nourishment ministered, and knit together, increaseth with the increase of God.

NOTES

Complete in Christ

Lesson Text: Colossians 2:6-19

Related Scriptures: John 10:22-33; Romans 6:1-12

TIME: A.D. 60   PLACE: from Rome

GOLDEN TEXT—"Ye are complete in him, which is the head of all principality and power" (Colossians 2:10).

Lesson Exposition

As Paul wrote to the Colossians, he told them that the secret to spiritual success is living on the basis of what Christ has already done for His people.

COMMITTED TO CHRIST—Col. 2:6-8

Walking in Christ (Col. 2:6). Paul was confident that the Colossians had gotten off to a good start in their Christian lives. They had heard and accepted the good news of salvation in Christ.

Nevertheless, it is possible for Christians to lose their spiritual focus. This was a particular danger in Colossae, because false teachers were threatening to damage the Christians.

The false teachers preached a new message with a diminished view of Christ. Paul challenged the Christians to walk in Christ, that is, maintain steady, faithful obedience to Him.

Built upon Christ (Col. 2:7). Paul continued by using several metaphors to describe how the Colossians were to keep growing in Christ. They were already rooted in Christ because they had a living relationship with Him.

Shifting the picture from a farm to a building, Paul said that in the present, the Colossians needed to be faithful so that they would be built up in Christ.

The false teachers claimed to offer an improved version of Christianity. But believers who are truly grateful for Christ's work will not desire to sample something that claims to be better.

Taught by Christ (Col. 2:8). Paul warned about the danger of "philosophy and vain deceit." He did not reject the use of philosophy as such, for he used a philosophic approach with the intellectuals in Athens (Acts 17:22-31). Believers should recognize that clear thinking is ennobling and constructive, but man-centered thinking that rejects Christ is vain, empty illusion. Everything we hear and read must be measured by what God has taught in His Word and through Christ.

COMPLETE IN CHRIST—Col. 2:9-15

Christ's deity (Col. 2:9). The human traditions that the false teachers in Colossae proclaimed diminished the significance of Jesus Christ. Paul countered their erroneous claims by emphasizing that Christ is, in fact, fully divine. The false teachers apparently contended that Christ was one of many intermediate beings that come between God and humans. Paul reasserted that in Christ the fullness of the Godhead, or complete deity, dwells.

Christ's authority (Col. 2:10). No doubt the false teachers said that the Christians needed some kind of ritual in addition to Christ in order to fully satisfy God's requirements. Paul reassured them that Christ was all they needed. By His perfection as the God-Man, He fully satisfied God's righteous demands when He died on the cross. Those who have received His gift of salvation are complete in Him.

Christ's sufficiency (Col. 2:11). The rite of circumcision was the distinguishing sign of the covenant between the Lord and the family of Abraham (cf. Gen. 17). Paul argued strongly that in Christ, believers have received a spiritual circumcision that surpasses the physical circumcision of the Old Testament law.

Christ's resurrection (Col. 2:12-13). As circumcision pictured the special relationship between God and Israel in the Old Testament, so baptism pictures the special relationship between Christ and the church in the New Testament. Baptism is a picture of the identification of the believer with Christ in His death, burial, and resurrection.

Christ's triumph (Col. 2:14-15). The false teachers in Colossae taught that the law was a necessary addition to what Christ had done. Paul explained that in reality, Christ's death blotted out, or made obsolete, the Mosaic Law, which condemned us. It was as if the law itself were nailed to the cross.

The false teachers also revered various orders of spiritual beings, which they taught were intermediaries between God and humans. Christ's resurrection, however, sealed His triumph over all the forces of evil. To worship angels, either good or evil, would direct attention to beings that are clearly inferior to Christ.

CONTENT IN CHRIST—Col. 2:16-19

Reality in Christ (Col. 2:16-17). As Paul countered the false teachers in Colossae, he reminded the Christians of the preeminence of Christ.

The Colossian heretics emphasized external activities, such as dietary restrictions and special worship days, instead of focusing on Christ Himself. Paul said that the religious rites were like a shadow compared with Christ.

Vitality in Christ (Col. 2:18-19). The false teachers claimed to have special knowledge that was unavailable to others. In their pride, they looked down on the believers.

Paul reminded the believers that Christ alone holds together both the universe and the church. Only by holding fast to Christ can Christians increase in their spiritual vitality.

—*Daniel J. Estes.*

QUESTIONS

1. What did Paul mean by the phrase "walk ye in him" (Col. 2:6)?
2. Why is gratitude an important preventative against error?
3. How did Paul regard human philosophy both positively and negatively?
4. Why did Paul emphasize the deity of Christ as he countered false teaching?
5. Why could Christ alone satisfy the righteous demands of God?
6. Why was the rite of circumcision so important to Jews in the Old Testament period?
7. How does baptism picture what Christ has done for Christians?
8. How did Paul illustrate that the law is now obsolete for Christians?
9. What did the false teachers in Colossae focus on?
10. Why did the false teachers look down on the Colossian Christians?

—*Daniel J. Estes.*

PRACTICAL POINTS

1. The Christian life is to be characterized by consistency, stability, and a spirit of thanksgiving (Col. 2:6-7).
2. Any teaching that deviates at all from the truth of Christ's deity must be rejected (vss. 8-9).
3. When we are grounded in the truth that we are complete in Christ, false teaching will have no appeal to us (vss. 10-14).
4. As Christians, we need not live in fear of Satan and his demons; they are defeated foes (vs. 15).
5. To adopt the legalistic observances some people would demand of us is to abandon our freedom in Christ (vss. 16-17).
6. Let us not heed anyone who elevates a person or an experience to the same level as Christ (vss. 18-19).

—Jarl K. Waggoner.

RESEARCH AND DISCUSSION

1. What elements are necessary for a person to be rooted and built up in Christ (Col. 2:7)? Is your church doing a good job in promoting spiritual growth?
2. Why do you think Paul wrote so much about the believer's relationship to sin as he dealt with false teaching (vss. 11-14)?
3. What should the Christian's attitude toward Satan be (Col. 2:15; cf. I Pet. 5:8-9)? What extremes must be avoided?
4. What characteristics of false teachers can you find in Colossians 2:16-19? How are these manifested in religious circles today?

—Jarl K. Waggoner.

Golden Text Illuminated

"Ye are complete in him, which is the head of all principality and power" (Colossians 2:10).

Part of why the gospel of Jesus Christ is such good news is that in Him we can experience true fullness, meaning, and purpose that will endure for all eternity. Christ is the God-Man. All of God's fullness is in Him. And when we turn to Christ in faith, we are brought into union with Him.

To truly understand this majestic verse, we must remember that the grand theme of Paul's letter to the Colossians is the preeminence of Christ. The key passage of the book is 1:15-18. In these verses we learn that Christ is the perfect image of God because He is God; that He is the Author of creation and that it has all been created for Him; and that He is also the Head of the church, which is the vanguard of the new creation that God brings into being to overcome the baleful effects that sin brought into the world (cf. Rom. 8:19-23). Why did the Father set things up this way? It was "that in all things [Christ] might have the preeminence" (Col. 1:18).

Christ is the Head. He has all authority, even over all the spiritual principalities that try to usurp God's rule.

Related to this truth is the glorious heart of the gospel, that we are free from the guilt and dominating power of sin. We are covered in Christ's righteousness, and the power of the risen Christ within us enables us to progressively conquer what sin remains as we grow more Christlike in our mind, heart, and will.

May we spend much time in grateful meditation on the inexhaustible riches of what it means to be complete in Christ.

—Stephen H. Barnhart.

LESSON 13 2/27/24   FEBRUARY 25, 2024

Scripture Lesson Text

PHM. 1:4 I thank my God, making mention of thee always in my prayers,

5 Hearing of thy love and faith, which thou hast toward the Lord Jesus, and toward all saints;

6 That the communication of thy faith may become effectual by the acknowledging of every good thing which is in you in Christ Jesus.

7 For we have great joy and consolation in thy love, because the bowels of the saints are refreshed by thee, brother.

8 Wherefore, though I might be much bold in Christ to enjoin thee that which is convenient,

9 Yet for love's sake I rather beseech *thee,* being such an one as Paul the aged, and now also a prisoner of Jesus Christ.

10 I beseech thee for my son Onesimus, whom I have begotten in my bonds:

11 Which in time past was to thee unprofitable, but now profitable to thee and to me:

12 Whom I have sent again: thou therefore receive him, that is, mine own bowels:

13 Whom I would have retained with me, that in thy stead he might have ministered unto me in the bonds of the gospel:

14 But without thy mind would I do nothing; that thy benefit should not be as it were of necessity, but willingly.

15 For perhaps he therefore departed for a season, that thou shouldest receive him for ever;

16 Not now as a servant, but above a servant, a brother beloved, specially to me, but how much more unto thee, both in the flesh, and in the Lord?

17 If thou count me therefore a partner, receive him as myself.

18 If he hath wronged thee, or oweth *thee* ought, put that on mine account;

19 I Paul have written *it* with mine own hand, I will repay *it:* albeit I do not say to thee how thou owest unto me even thine own self besides.

20 Yea, brother, let me have joy of thee in the Lord: refresh my bowels in the Lord.

21 Having confidence in thy obedience I wrote unto thee, knowing that thou wilt also do more than I say.

NOTES

A Plea for Christlike Forgiveness

Lesson Text: Philemon 1:4-21

Related Scriptures: Matthew 6:9-15; I Corinthians 16:13-14; III John 1:2-4

TIME: A.D. 60   PLACE: from Rome

GOLDEN TEXT—"Be ye kind one to another, tenderhearted, forgiving one another, even as God for Christ's sake hath forgiven you" (Ephesians 4:32).

Lesson Exposition

COMMENDATION OF PHILEMON—Phm. 1:4-7

Praise for Philemon's ministry (Phm. 1:4-5). Philemon had opened his home to other Christians. As Paul thought of his striking example of godliness, he thanked God for him.

Prayer for Philemon's progress (Phm. 1:6). Paul longed for Philemon to keep developing in practical godliness. He spoke of Philemon's "communication" of his faith. Paul was going to ask him to move to the next level of godliness by forgiving his runaway slave, Onesimus.

Proof of Philemon's love (Phm. 1:7). Philemon had a record of compassion in action. Many of the believers in Colossae had been nourished by his loving provision. Paul derived great joy and encouragement from him.

COMPASSION FOR ONESIMUS—Phm. 1:8-16

Basis for Paul's appeal (Phm. 1:8-9). Runaway slaves had no rights at all. They were subject to whatever punishment the master determined to exact, up to and including death. Paul was going to ask Philemon to take a public stand against the cultural norm.

As an apostle, Paul had been given authority in the church by Christ. Paul knew that he could use this position to put pressure on Philemon to accept Onesimus.

In this case, however, Paul appealed on a different basis. Instead of bearing down on Philemon's sense of duty, Paul's appeal endeavored to touch his heart and prompt a loving response.

Paul referred to himself as "Paul the aged" (vs. 9). Paul was probably about sixty years old at this time. In addition, Paul mentioned his present imprisonment for Christ.

Blessing of Onesimus's change (Phm. 1:10-11). God had accomplished a wonderful transformation in Onesimus's life. Paul described this runaway slave as his spiritual child in the faith. When Onesimus had run away from Colossae, the Lord had directed his steps to Paul in his confinement, where Paul had led him to Christ.

Since that time, Onesimus's life had changed dramatically.

Benefit of Onesimus's ministry (Phm. 1:12-13). No doubt Onesimus himself carried this letter from Paul to his master, Philemon. This return was painful, for Onesimus knew well how runaway slaves were commonly treated by their masters. Paul also found it difficult, for he had come to love this new Christian, who had ministered to him during his imprisonment.

Onesimus was, in effect, functioning as Philemon's servant by doing for Paul just what his master would have commanded him to do. Paul nevertheless knew that the only right thing to do was to send Onesimus back to Philemon.

Boundary of Paul's action (Phm. 1:14). Paul did not presume to command Philemon as to what he should do. Although he used persuasion and emotion to move Philemon, he did not step over the line of what was proper in order to get Philemon to receive Onesimus.

Bond of Christian love (Phm. 1:15-16). In God's family, relationships are not limited by time. Philemon had lost temporarily the services of a slave, but he had received something far better. By God's miraculous grace, Onesimus was now a beloved brother both to Paul and to his master, Philemon.

CONFIDENCE OF PAUL—
Phm. 1:17-21

Firm relationship (Phm. 1:17). Knowing that Philemon regarded him as a partner in Christ, Paul urged him to receive Onesimus in the same way that he would receive Paul.

Financial resources (Phm. 1:18-19). Onesimus's absence had substantial financial implications. At the very least, Philemon had lost his services. It is also likely that he took money or other items. Paul volunteered to pay anything that Onesimus owed Philemon. To make this offer official, Paul wrote this letter in his own handwriting.

As Paul confirmed his willingness to assume the debts of Onesimus, he also gently reminded Philemon of the even greater debt that he owed the apostle. Apparently Paul had been a significant influence in bringing him to faith in Christ.

Faithful response (Phm. 1:20-21). By receiving Onesimus, Philemon could bring joy and refreshment to the imprisoned Paul.

Paul was confident that Philemon would act as he had requested. In fact, Paul suspected that he would go even further.

—*Daniel J. Estes.*

QUESTIONS

1. Why did Paul think so highly of Philemon?
2. How did Paul challenge Philemon to advance in godliness?
3. How had Philemon already demonstrated God's love at work through his life?
4. What was the status of runaway slaves in the first-century Roman world?
5. On what basis did Paul appeal to Philemon?
6. How had Onesimus been useful to Paul?
7. How far did Paul go in his request, and where did he stop in urging Philemon?
8. In what way did Philemon receive back a different Onesimus?
9. How did Paul offer to stand behind Onesimus?
10. In what way was Philemon indebted to Paul?

—*Daniel J. Estes.*

PRACTICAL POINTS

1. We can show no greater appreciation for a person than to pray for him (Phm. 1:4-5).
2. When love marks our lives, we will be a great encouragement to our fellow Christians (vss. 6-7).
3. We are wise to appeal to our brethren on the basis of Christian love, our highest motivation (vss. 8-9).
4. The transforming power of the Christian faith produces profitable service from those who were useless (vss. 10-13).
5. God can bring good even from the evil acts of people (vss. 14-16).
6. A new Christian is as much a part of God's family as a mature saint and should be accepted as such (vss. 17-19).
7. We who have received God's forgiveness should be eager to show kindness to others (vss. 20-21).

—Jarl K. Waggoner.

RESEARCH AND DISCUSSION

1. What was the essence of Paul's prayers for Philemon (Phm. 1:4-6)? How does this compare to what we pray for others?
2. What can you determine about the character and history of Onesimus and Philemon from this short book?
3. What evidence do you see of God's providential working in the life of Onesimus?
4. How did Paul's appeal to Philemon illustrate his own teaching in other epistles (cf. Eph. 6:5-9)? What do you think was the likely outcome of Onesimus's return to Philemon?

—Jarl K. Waggoner.

Golden Text Illuminated

"Be ye kind one to another, tenderhearted, forgiving one another, even as God for Christ's sake hath forgiven you" (Ephesians 4:32).

The text before us is a difficult one. The difficulty is not in the area of understanding. We all know what the text says. The problem is in putting the command found here into practice. It is not easy to treat others the same way God has dealt with us in Christ.

God has treated the believer with unconditional love. He has forgiven the Christian with no strings attached. "If we confess our sins, he is faithful and just to forgive us our sins, and to cleanse us from all unrighteousness" (I John 1:9).

God calls His children to treat each other in the same way. He tells us our relationships must be marked by this kind of tenderness and willingness to forgive.

An unforgiving spirit nullifies our testimony. It lets others know that we do not understand the forgiveness that is offered to us in Jesus Christ.

Our example is God. We are not to compare ourselves with each other. We are not to base our actions on how others treat us. God is to be the standard we measure ourselves against.

We have not been called to merely put up with people; we have been commanded to treat them with kindness and tenderness. These are attitudes that are focused on meeting the needs of others and not our own selfish desires.

Much strife in the church could be avoided if professing Christians would follow Christ's example. It is hard to quarrel and bicker with someone you stand ready to forgive.

—James R. Gordon.

PARAGRAPHS ON PLACES AND PEOPLE

ROME

The Christian faith may have first been brought to Rome by converts who were at Jerusalem during Pentecost (Acts 2:10, 41). Rome, located on the Italian peninsula, was the capital of the Roman Empire, which ruled a vast territory during Paul's ministry. It encompassed the Mediterranean Sea from the Middle East to southern Europe, Britain, North Africa, Asia Minor, and beyond. In Jerusalem, when Paul was about to be scourged, he asserted his Roman citizenship even though he was born in Tarsus, a city in Asia Minor over a thousand miles from Rome.

Paul's prison letters were written from Rome. During his lifetime, Christianity spread throughout the empire—the known world in the first century (Col. 1:6). Emperor Nero oversaw the first definitive persecution of Christians by the imperial power. It is widely believed that Paul was beheaded in Rome under Nero.

EPHESUS

Paul had an extended ministry in Ephesus, but he also got into trouble there. His message against idols was bad for local business (Acts 19:26-27).

Ephesus, located in western Asia Minor, was an extremely idolatrous city. It was home to the temple to Diana, one of the seven wonders of the ancient world (vs. 35). Today it is one of the most excavated sites in the world.

Ephesus may have had the most prominent church outside of Jerusalem. The city is referenced nine times in Acts and six times in Paul's epistles. Paul wrote I Corinthians from Ephesus (16:8), and his letter to the Ephesians was most likely a general epistle written for more than one church.

ONESIMUS

Onesimus was a slave, who after running away from his master, Philemon, in Colossae, was converted by the apostle Paul in Rome. Onesimus became an effective aide to Paul during his Roman imprisonment. Onesimus's name—meaning "profitable" (Phm. 1:11)—is mentioned in verse 10 and Colossians 4:9.

In a personal letter to Philemon, Paul draws on Philemon's current relationship with Onesimus to appeal for a new one, urging him to receive Onesimus back as a Christian brother and no longer as a slave (vs. 16). In this appeal Paul illustrates redemption (vs. 18), unity and equality in Christ, and voluntary servanthood in contrast with slavery (Phm. 1:13; cf. Gal. 3:28).

EPAPHRODITUS

Epaphroditus's name (meaning "agreeable") is mentioned only in Paul's letter to the Philippian church (2:25; 4:18). They had sent him to aid Paul in various ways, not least materially. But Epaphroditus, while in Rome, had become deathly ill. He was so concerned about his fellow Philippians that Paul sent him back earlier than intended so he could reassure them about his condition (2:25-30).

Paul also sent him back so he could minister to the Philippians while Paul and Timothy's visit was delayed (vss. 19-25). Though Paul benefited from Epaphroditus's presence, he put the man's ministry to others ahead of his own needs.

—*Brian Burke.*

Daily Bible Readings for Home Study and Worship

(Readings are for the week previous to the lesson topics.)

1. December 3.   To Live Is Christ
M — Macedonian Call. Acts 16:9-13.
T — Powerful Ministry in Philippi. Acts 16:14-18.
W — Opposition Defeated in Philippi. Acts 16:19-40.
T — Prayer for the Philippians. Phil. 1:1-11.
F — God Works All Things for Good. Rom. 8:26-28.
S — Eternity with the Lord. II Cor. 5:1-9.
S — A Godly Perspective on Life and Death. Phil. 1:12-26.

2. December 10.   Counting All Things Loss
M — Take Up Your Cross. Matt. 16:24-28.
T — A Living Hope. I Pet. 1:3-9.
W — Imitators of the Lord. I Thess. 1:2-10.
T — Fix Your Eyes on Jesus. Heb. 12:1-2.
F — Righteousness by Faith. Rom. 9:30—10:4.
S — The Crown of Righteousness. II Tim. 4:1-8.
S — Pressing On. Phil. 3:7-21.

3. December 17.   Learning Contentment
M — Abiding in Christ. John 15:1-8.
T — Content with What We Have. Heb. 13:5-8.
W — Supplying a Need. II Cor. 8:1-15.
T — The Blessing of Giving. II Cor. 9:1-15.
F — Contentment in Suffering. II Cor. 12:7-10.
S — Seek God's Kingdom. Luke 12:22-31.
S — The Secret to Contentment. Phil. 4:4-18.

4. December 24.   The Light of Christmas (Christmas)
M — God's Peace Ruling Our Hearts. Col. 3:12-17.
T — Love—the Sign of a Disciple. John 13:34-35.
W — The Darkness of the Wicked. II Tim. 3:1-9.
T — Walk in the Light. I John 1:5-7.
F — Grace-filled Speech. Col. 4:2-6.
S — Living a Holy Life. I Thess. 4:1-12.
S — Christ Brings Light and Life. John 1:1-5; Eph. 5:1-2, 6-14.

5. December 31.   Chosen in Christ
M — Paul Arrives in Ephesus. Acts 18:18-23.
T — Later Ministry in Ephesus. Acts 19:1-20.
W — Opposition in Ephesus. Acts 19:21—20:1.
T — Farewell to the Ephesian Elders. Acts 20:17-38.
F — Chosen by God. II Thess. 2:13-17.
S — Sealed by the Spirit. II Cor. 1:18-22.
S — An Eternal Plan. Eph. 1:3-14.

6. January 7.   God's Workmanship
M — Justified by Faith. Rom. 3:20-31.
T — Cleansing Needed. Ps. 51:1-12.
W — Back from the Dead. Luke 15:11-24.
T — The Riches of Grace. Eph. 3:1-12.
F — Not by Works. Titus 3:1-7.
S — Equipped for Good Works. II Tim. 3:14-17.
S — Created for Good Works. Eph. 2:1-10.

7. January 14.   The Household of God
M — Many Members—One Body. Rom. 12:3-8.
T — Sons by Faith. Gal. 3:26-29.
W — Strangers Will Join the People of God. Matt. 8:5-11.
T — Teach Your Children About God. Ps. 78:5-8.
F — Sheep from Another Fold. John 10:14-18.
S — Jews and Gentiles Called by God. Rom. 9:22-26.
S — Christ Makes Us One. Eph. 2:11-22.

8. January 21.   A High Calling
M — Baptized into One Body. I Cor. 12:12-20.
T — The United Body of Christ. I Cor. 12:21-31.
W — Unity of Mind. I Pet. 3:8-12.
T — God Reigns from Mount Zion. Ps. 68:15-18.
F — Christ's Eternal Glory. John 17:4-5.
S — Ultimate Humility—Ultimate Exaltation. Phil. 2:5-11.
S — Unity of Faith. Eph. 4:1-16.

9. January 28.   God-Honoring Families
M — God Instituted Marriage. Matt. 19:4-6.
T — God-Ordained Roles in Marriage. I Pet. 3:1-7.
W — God Rules over All Relationships. I Cor. 11:3, 11-12.
T — An Exemplary Wife. Prov. 31:10-12, 23, 26-29.
F — Vital Principles for Christian Families. Col. 3:18-21.
S — Imparting Wisdom to Children. Prov. 3:1-2.
S — Submitting to One Another. Eph. 5:21—6:4.

10. February 4.   Spiritual Armor
M — A Deadly Enemy. I Pet. 5:6-11.
T — A Spiritual Battle. Dan. 10:10-21.
W — Pray for All People. I Tim. 2:1-4.
T — Submit to God. Jas. 4:1-10.
F — Spiritual Weapons. II Cor. 10:1-5.
S — Power of God's Word. Luke 4:1-13.
S — Prepare for Battle. Eph. 6:10-24.

11. February 11.   The Supremacy of Christ
M — Jesus and the Father Are One. John 14:9-11.
T — Through Him Are All Things. I Cor. 8:4-6.
W — Christ—the Firstfruits of Resurrection Life. I Cor. 15:20-28.
T — Jesus, the Alpha and the Omega. Rev. 1:4-8.
F — The Fullness of God. John 1:14-18.
S — Reconciled Through Christ. II Cor. 5:17-21.
S — Christ's Greatness. Col. 1:15-28.

12. February 18.   Complete in Christ
M — Jesus Is God. John 10:24-33.
T — United with Christ. Rom. 6:1-12.
W — Beware of False Teaching. I Tim. 4:1-8.
T — Beware of Traditions of Men. Matt. 15:1-9.
F — Christ Does What the Law Could Not Do. Rom. 7:1-6.
S — Treasures of Wisdom in Christ. Col. 2:1-5.
S — Christ Is the Head. Col. 2:6-19.

13. February 25.   A Plea for Christlike Forgiveness
M — Ministering to the Saints. Heb. 6:9-12.
T — Refreshing the Saints. I Cor. 16:13-18.
W — The Refreshment of a Faithful Testimony. III John 1:2-4.
T — Useful in Ministry. Phil. 2:19, 22-30; II Tim. 4:11.
F — Appeal for Reconciliation. Phil. 4:1-3.
S — Forgive Our Debtors. Matt. 6:9-15.
S — Forgiveness and Acceptance. Phm. 1:4-21.